GREAT BRITISH CHEESES

GREAT BRITISH CHEESES

JENNY LINFORD

London, New York, Munich,
Melbourne, Delhi

Project Editor Daniel Mills
Senior Art Editor Sara Robin
Executive Managing Editor Adèle Hayward
Managing Art Editor Kat Mead
Senior Production Editor Jenny Woodcock
Production Controller Alice Holloway
Creative Technical Support Sonia Charbonnier
Art Director Peter Luff
Publisher Stephanie Jackson

Produced for DK by
Dawn Bates (Editor) and Emma Forge (Designer)
Production Designer Tom Forge
Photography by Will Heap

First published in Great Britain in 2008
by Dorling Kindersley Limited,
80 Strand, London WC2R 0RL

A Penguin Company

2 4 6 8 10 9 7 5 3 1

Copyright © 2008 Dorling Kindersley Ltd

A CIP catalogue record for this book is
available from the British Library.
ISBN: 978 1 4053 3436 5
Reproduced by MDP, Bath, UK
Printed and bound in China by L-Rex

Discover more at
www.dk.com

"To the cheesemakers
and cheesemongers
of Britain and Ireland,
in appreciation of
their hard work
and dedication."

CONTENTS

INTRODUCTION

CHEESE IS ONE OF THOSE FOODS that arouses strong feelings in those who make, sell, and eat it – an everyday food that people feel passionately about. Luckily for those who love cheese, the cheese-making scene in Britain and Ireland today has an energy and vibrancy to it. Both countries have seen a huge surge in traditional, artisanal cheese-making since the late 1970s, in happy contrast to the dramatic decline experienced during the decades following World War II.

What is so striking about current British and Irish cheese-making is its creativity. While traditional, much-loved favourites, such as Cheddar, Stilton, and Lancashire, still thankfully exist, a huge number of modern cheeses are being freshly created by cheesemakers, many of whom have only recently started in the industry. Britain has always been known for its hard cheeses, for classics such as Cheshire or Wensleydale. Today, however, cheesemakers in Britain and in Ireland are creating a whole range of different textured cheeses: pungent-smelling, semi-soft washed-rind cheeses, fragile fresh cheeses, creamy blues, and melt-in-the-mouth soft cheeses.

CREATIVE CHEESE-MAKING

Traditional methods are still respectfully embraced by many cheesemakers, but these sit alongside a willingness to be creative and inventive. Whereas once cow's milk was the norm for British cheeses, today's cheesemakers are using goat's, sheep's, and even buffalo's milk to make everything from hard to blue cheeses. The result of this vitality is great diversity in the cheeses of Britain and Ireland. To see this most clearly, look around a cheesemonger's shop at the wide variety of British and Irish cheeses on offer; these are the tangible, edible evidence that cheese lovers in Britain and in Ireland are living in exciting times.

Cheese-making is an intricate process, requiring a careful eye for detail and scrupulous hygiene. Seasonal variations in the milk have a direct impact on the cheese, affecting flavour and texture. While some cheesemakers take milk from their own livestock as their starting point, others have to work with bought-in milk, and ensuring a steady, reliable source can be problematic. The cheesemakers at the forefront of Britain's cheese revival in the 1970s and 1980s faced additional

Britain's artisan cheese industry is now more vibrant than ever. The number of entries at the British Cheese Awards has trebled since 1994 and continues to grow every year.

DIVERSE AND ORIGINAL
The sheer variety of available colours, shapes, flavours, and textures is evidence of just how creative the contemporary British and Irish cheese industry has become.

challenges. Those using unpasteurized, or raw, milk were often treated with suspicion by public health inspectors, and health scares, misreported and exaggerated by the media, had dire consequences for fledgling dairies. Where cheeses made using sheep's or goat's milk barely register as novelties today, in the 1980s they were often regarded with suspicion or just a lack of interest. In making new cheeses from unconventional ingredients, these artisans were breaking new ground and had to create a market for their produce. Cheesemakers today still face problems, but fortunately the overall climate is far more receptive to and supportive of farmhouse cheeses, thanks to these early pioneers.

Unlike in France, with its established tradition of classic cheeses, many of them legally defined by a system of regulation, cheesemakers in Britain are far more individualistic. The pioneering wave of cheesemakers who revived farmhouse cheese-making continues to be joined by many new enthusiasts, who also find themselves drawn to the fascination, challenges, and satisfaction of making cheese.

REGIONAL CHEESE-MAKING

Classic, "territorial" cheeses such as Cheddar, Lancashire, and Cheshire, were often named after the areas in which they were produced, and a sense of place is still important to many cheesemakers. Locally sourced, raw milk is considered to be an expression of the landscape – the soil, the grass, and the bacteria – and as a cheese ripens, it is uniquely flavoured by naturally occurring microbes in the surrounding environment. The salty Cheshire plains, for example, are said to give a distinctive tang to the milk of cattle grazed there, and to the cheese made from it. The humid climate of the south-west of Ireland is valued by local cheesemakers for favouring washed-rind cheeses such as Gubbeen, made in County Cork. The map opposite shows the regional boundaries that historically have defined British and Irish cheeses, many of which follow traditional county borders.

ABOUT THIS BOOK

Great British Cheeses is a guide to the wealth of British and Irish cheeses now available. I've tried to give a sense of the flavour of each cheese, and the history behind it, as well as the manufacturing techniques that make every cheese unique. Hand-made cheeses vary from batch to batch in taste, texture, and size, so the measurements given are approximate guidelines. For the shapes of the cheeses, I have used the descriptions given by the producers.

Researching this book has been a fascinating experience, and has brought home to me the sheer dedication and hard work that goes into every piece of artisanal cheese. I have talked to cheesemakers from the remote Isle of Mull to the green pastures of County Cork, and had the pleasure of tasting their cheeses. I hope this book will offer guidance and encouragement to cheese lovers to further explore and enjoy the great variety of cheeses on offer.

Jenny Linford

The best artisanal cheeses carry with them a sense of history, expressing the climate, landscape, and agricultural heritage of the regions that produce them.

BRITISH AND IRISH CHEESE-MAKING REGIONS

A SHORT HISTORY
OF BRITISH CHEESE

BRITAIN'S LUSH, GREEN MEADOWS have long been valued as pasture for livestock, particularly sheep and cows. For centuries, these animals have been a vital source of meat, wool, leather, and milk. The Romans, who invaded Britain in 43AD and occupied it for nearly 400 years, are credited with bringing their extensive dairy knowledge to Britain, and cheese-making may be part of their legacy.

Hundreds of years later, French Cistercian monks, who came over with William the Conqueror and settled in the Yorkshire Dales, passed on their knowledge of cheese-making to the local community, establishing a tradition in the Dales that continues to this very day.

Sheep's milk was favoured for early cheese-making in Britain, but over the centuries the cow became the islands' major dairy animal, valued for its high milk yield and the ease with which its milk could be turned into butter. For centuries, British cheese-making was very much a farmhouse activity, and cheeses were mostly made during the summer when milk was abundant. Traditionally, cheese-making was a female preserve, undertaken by the farmer's wife and the dairymaid, who passed the skills and knowledge on from mother to daughter.

By the 17th century, a number of so-called "territorial" cheeses were well established in England, named after the part of the country in which they were made. Cheshire is the earliest known English cheese, mentioned in the Domesday Book of 1086AD, while other regional cheeses included Cheddar, Stilton, Derby, Leicester, and Lancashire. With transport slow and unreliable, and no refrigeration, cheese was the only way to preserve excess milk for sale in commercial centres such as London.

THE IMPACT OF INDUSTRIALIZATION

Rural cheese-making began to suffer with the advent of the Industrial Revolution in the 18th and 19th centuries. The coming of the railways meant that farmers could now send surplus milk into towns and cities in liquid form. The British cheese industry itself began to move towards mechanization and mass production in 1870, with the opening of England's first purpose-built cheese factory at Longford, near Derby,

Cheese-making techniques have been honed over centuries, evolving from a basic method of preserving milk into a skilled craft, producing some of Britain and Ireland's finest foods.

GOOD LIVESTOCK

British cheese-making has always depended on the islands' lush pastures. Well-nourished animals produce excess milk, giving rise to a strong tradition of dairy farming and cheese production.

making Derby cheese. This process of industrialization continued in the early 20th century, with large-scale factory production becoming increasingly common. World War I (1914–18), with its accompanying mass slaughter of men of working age, had a devastating impact on British farming. The 1920s and 1930s saw a deep agricultural depression, leading to the creation by the government in 1933 of the Milk Marketing Board, an organization that offered dairy farmers a guaranteed market for their milk and their cheese.

DECLINE IN CHEESE PRODUCTION

World War II (1939–45) dealt further blows to farmhouse cheese-making in Britain. Prompted by an understandable anxiety to ensure food supplies, the government took centralized control of food production. The Ministry of Food was created in 1939, and among its decrees was one which was to have a devastating impact on traditional British cheese-making. This was the decision that only a handful of hard cheeses could be made: Cheddar, Cheshire, Dunlop, Scottish Cheddar, Leicester, and a hard Wensleydale. Traditional cheeses, including Stilton, Gloucester, Lancashire, and Caerphilly, were no longer to be produced. Furthermore, cheese was rationed, and it was to be 1954 before it became freely available once again. Figures for farmhouse cheese production in this period make depressing reading. In Cheshire, 405 farms made their own cheese in 1939; by 1948, this figure had been cut to 44. Farmhouse cheesemakers in the South-West declined from 514 before World War II to just 61 afterwards.

This decline continued during the decades following the end of World War II. In the 1960s, supermarkets became the dominant force in British food retailing, selling mostly block cheeses, pre-packed and sealed in plastic. Instead of character and flavour, cheapness, uniformity, and ease of production were the main requirements. Moist cheeses, which required care to mature well, were rejected in favour of hard cheeses that could be sold young. The lack of legal protection for British cheeses, in contrast to France's system of *Appelations d'origine contrôlée* (see page 157) with its rules defining farming practice and methods of production, made it easy to produce debased versions of many traditional cheeses.

The risks and hard work that went into reviving British and Irish cheese-making in the 1970s and '80s have paid off, and cheese-lovers today are reaping the rewards.

TRANSPORTING CHEESE
Hard cheeses were valued as a food that travelled
well. Transporting cheeses to market became easier
with the advent of the railways and the motor car.

A BRIGHTER FUTURE

If British and Irish cheese-making hit rock bottom in the 1960s, the 1970s saw the
beginnings of a renaissance. Farmhouse cheesemakers, ignored by the supermarkets,
suddenly found a new market in the form of specialist cheese shops such as Patrick
Rance's Wells Stores in Streatley, James Aldridge's shop James's in Beckenham, and
Randolph Hodgson's Neal's Yard Dairy in London. Rance, Aldridge, and Hodgson,
driven by the realization that this great food tradition was in danger of extinction,
worked with producers to develop high-quality products, while their stores and, later,
farmers markets provided an outlet for the cheeses and helped to develop a discerning
clientele. Traditional cheeses were re-created and new varieties were invented. Several
organizations were set up to protect and promote artisan cheesemakers: the Irish
Farmhouse Cheesemakers Association (CAIS) in 1983, the Specialist Cheesemakers
Association in Britain in 1989, and the British Cheese Awards (see page 185) in 1994.

The effect has been dramatic. Today, the Specialist Cheesemakers Association has
more than 300 members. In its first year, the British Cheese Awards had fewer than
300 entries; now the figure is close to 900. Making cheese still involves relentless hard
work and is often beset with uncertainty; however, with an increasing number of
consumers demonstrating an appetite for high-quality, locally produced, traceable
food, the future for British and Irish cheeses looks bright.

HOW CHEESE IS MADE

CHEESEMAKERS USE A WIDE VARIETY OF TECHNIQUES to create the vast array of cheeses on offer – from meltingly soft blue cheeses, veined with mould, to the robust hard cheeses so typical of Britain's cheese heritage. It is a tribute to the ingenuity and inventiveness of cheesemakers, of both the past and today, that from the same basic liquid ingredient, milk, so many different types of cheese can be produced.

FROM MILK TO CHEESE

It is milk, of course, that defines the make-up of cheese: fat gives texture and flavour; an elastic protein called casein links together to form the curd; and lactose, the major milk sugar, provides energy for the bacteria that begin the fermentation process.

The milk from different dairy animals has its own characteristics: cow's milk, for example, has large fat globules that rise to the surface and a firm casein structure, while goat's milk is naturally partially homogenized, with smaller fat particles. There are further differences between the milks of different breeds of the same animal. For example, the milk from Jersey or Guernsey cows is far higher in fat than that produced by Friesian cows. Even the milk from a single animal varies in quality and composition according to the animal's diet, the time of year, the stage the animal has reached in its lactation period, and the time of day the animal is milked. Good-quality milk is therefore vital to cheesemakers, and, while some use milk from their own livestock others have to find a reliable supplier, which is not always easy.

STAGES OF PRODUCTION

Broadly speaking, there are four stages of production that are needed to transform milk into any type of cheese.

• **Controlling acidity levels:** The first step is to raise the acidity levels of the milk by converting some of the lactose to lactic acid. Historically, this was simply done by leaving the milk to "turn", allowing naturally occuring bacteria to work. Many cheese-makers today, however, work with milk that has been pasteurized (a process which eliminates both harmful and beneficial bacteria), so this stage is now usually achieved by adding a "starter culture" of the desired bacteria.

Many of the techniques used by today's cheesemakers date back centuries, while modern technology allows ever finer control of the conditions that create a cheese's unique flavour.

FORMING CURD

Raising the acidity level is the first step in separating the liquid component of milk (whey) from the solid curd that will go on to form the cheese.

• **Curdling:** The milk is then curdled, a process that separates the solids (mostly fat and protein) from the liquids (mostly water) within the milk. Usually this is done by adding rennet (see page 67), a natural substance which contains the digestive enzyme rennin (also known as chymosin). Rennin acts on the natural milk protein, casein, causing it to coagulate into solid curd. The traditional source of rennet is the lining of the fourth stomach of a calf, although rennin can be found in the stomachs of other young animals. For centuries, strips of dried stomach lining were used to curdle milk.

Today's cheesemakers can use either animal rennet or vegetarian, or genetically engineered equivalents extracted from plants or moulds. The soured milk is heated, and the rennet is added in the form of a liquid or powder. The milk begins to separate into curd and whey, the curd being the coagulated fat and protein, and the whey being the watery part of the milk. How the curd is treated affects the final texture of the cheese – it may simply be gently ladled into moulds, to give a fresh, moist cheese, or it may be cut or passed through a mill, processes that help to expel the whey, resulting in a drier, harder cheese.

• **Moulding and shaping:** The curd is then formed into cheeses by being placed into moulds to drain. The Italian word for cheese, *formaggio*, and the French for cheese, *fromage*, both derive from the Latin word *forma*, meaning "to mould or

PRESSING CHEESES
Using a cheese press helps to remove any whey in the curd and to shape the cheese. The extent to which a press is used affects the final texture.

shape", which referred to the wicker baskets used to drain cheeses. The diversity of sizes and shapes of cheese reflects the possibilities available to the cheesemaker at this stage. The rinds of many cheeses carry the imprint of the moulds in which they were formed. Different textures can be achieved by leaving the curd to drain naturally under its own weight or by pressing it to drive out moisture.

• **Maturing:** In this final stage of the process, the young cheese is aged in an environment that best suits its development. Cheeses that retain a lot of moisture in the curd, for example, are matured for less time than those with a dry curd. Soft cheeses require only a short ripening time of a few days before they are ready to eat. Mould-ripened cheeses are placed in a warm, humid atmosphere to encourage the development of mould on the surface and inside. Once the initial shape has been achieved through moulding, some cheeses are wrapped in cloth, sealed with lard, and matured; this is especially true of large hard cheeses such as a classic farmhouse Cheddar. This process allows the cheese to develop in flavour and texture, and to form a rind that will protect the paste.

Factory-made hard cheeses are wrapped in a plastic coating which allows the cheese to mature faster, but without developing any mould or rind. The resulting "block" cheese has a softer curd because far less moisture is lost in this process than through the traditional process of cloth-wrapped maturing.

TESTING CHEESE
A cheese iron enables the cheesemaker to assess the progress of a maturing cheese without cutting it. Samples can be removed, tested, and replaced.

TYPES OF CHEESE

CHEESES CAN BE VERY BROADLY CATEGORIZED by texture – soft, semi-soft, and hard – and also by type – fresh and blue. Within these categories there are variations, but the names give an overall guideline to the sort of cheese you can expect to find.

FRESH CHEESES

As their name suggests, fresh cheeses are so young that they have no skin or mould. The cheesemaker ripens the milk, curdles it as for other cheeses, then carefully transfers the resulting curd into moulds. These are generally left to drain under their own weight, rather than by pressing, and are ready for sale in a matter of days. The resulting cheeses are characterized by their delicate, soft, easily spreadable paste and simple, clean taste.

Many fresh cheeses are flavoured with herbs, spices (such as black peppercorns), or flavourings such as garlic. These can be mixed into the curd or used as a decorative coating on the surface of the cheese.

SOFT CHEESES

This is a blanket term applied to younger cheeses with soft-textured paste. White mould-ripened cheeses are some of the most recognizable, characterized by a downy coating of *Penicillium candidum* mould across the rind. To achieve this effect, the cheesemaker generally adds *Penicillium* to the milk at the beginning of the cheese-making process and ensures that the curd remains moist in the mould. The shaped curd is then matured in a humid atmosphere, which encourages the growth of white *Penicillium* on the exterior of the cheese. The enzymes from this mould ripen the cheese from the outside in, softening its texture as they progress; white-mould cheeses tend to be flat and thin to aid this process.

Soft cheeses also include natural mould cheeses, where the cheesemaker, rather than introducing a specific, dominant mould into the milk, allows a coating of natural mould from the surrounding environment to develop. Often a coating of vegetable ash is applied to soft cheeses, particularly goat's cheeses, as it provides a favourable surface on which the moulds can develop.

Within each of the main cheese varieties – fresh, soft, semi-soft, hard, and blue – an astonishing variety of flavours waits to be explored, from smooth and buttery to tangy and spicy.

MOULD-RIPENED CHEESES
Many soft cheeses have a thin coating of white mould on their exterior, created by the addition of *Penicillium candidum* to the milk.

SEMI-SOFT CHEESES

Although semi-soft cheeses are characterized by a powerful, pungent odour, the actual flavour of the cheese is often mild in comparison to its smell. This category includes washed-rind cheeses, made by washing the rinds of the young cheese with brine or an alcoholic solution as they mature in order to encourage the growth of bacteria on the rind. The result is a distinctive sticky orange-brown exterior. As with the white *Penicillium*, the mould works its way from the outside in, causing the paste to soften voluptuously as it matures.

Washed-curd cheeses, also in this category, are made by washing the curd to arrest the process by which milk sugars are turned into lactic acid (see page 14). The resulting cheeses typically have a supple, pliable texture.

HARD CHEESES

Many of Britain's traditional favourites are hard cheeses, most notably Cheddar, but also varieties such as Caerphilly, Cheshire, Double Gloucester, Dunlop, Lancashire, and Wensleydale. Hard cheeses are aged for longer than any other type, in some cases maturing for several months. As a hard cheese develops, its flavour becomes more intense and complex, and its texture becomes drier and firmer. The investment of money and time required to make large hard cheeses is considerable. It takes around 300 litres (65 gallons) of milk, for example, to produce a 27kg (60lb) Cheddar using traditional methods.

The dense, firm texture of these cheeses is achieved by pressing (see page 15) during the manufacturing process. A huge variety of cheeses is included in this category, however, and their producers use a number of techniques to achieve different end products. These range from altering the temperature of the milk by as little as a degree, to using different methods to cut the curd, cutting the curd to different sizes, and applying varying degrees of pressure during pressing. All of these require careful judgement; too much pressure, for example, can cause the rind to split. Different methods of salting cheese also affect the final result. It is characteristic of the manufacture of many British hard cheeses for salt to be added to the curd at the end of the draining process, rather than it being added by immersing the cheese in brine.

Washed-rind cheeses include the smelliest varieties, such as the infamous Stinking Bishop, but you may be surprised by the mild, sweet flavours that lie behind their pungent odour.

Blue-green veining gives blue cheeses an easily identifiable look and flavour. It requires great skill to develop the mould correctly.

BLUE CHEESES

Historically, cheeses that were stored in cool, damp cellars or caves would naturally form a growth of mould from the bacteria in their surroundings. There are, therefore, "blue" versions of a number of traditional cheeses – for example, Blue Wensleydale and Blue Cheshire, the latter historically known locally as "green fade" cheese. Today, the makers of blue cheeses mix blue mould (usually *Penicillium roqueforti* or *Penicillium glaucum*) into the ripened milk. From then on, the whole process of making the cheese is designed to allow this mould to thrive and grow.

Blue cheeses are not usually pressed, in order to retain moisture and an open, airy texture in the curd, both of which encourage the mould to grow. To spread the moisture evenly, the cheeses are turned as they mature – many small-scale producers still do this by hand. Blue cheeses are traditionally matured in a warm, moist atmosphere that favours mould growth, and as an additional measure they are pierced with long needles as they mature, allowing air to penetrate the centre of the cheese. Mould develops along the paths left by the needles, forming the characteristic blue-green veining that spreads throughout the paste.

BUYING CHEESE

IT IS BEST TO BUY CHEESES from a reputable specialist cheesemonger – someone with a knowledge of the food they sell, who sources it carefully and handles it properly. A good cheesemonger will carry a wide range, giving you the chance to explore new varieties. The best cheesemongers allow you to taste the cheese before you buy it. Farmhouse cheeses can vary in flavour and texture due to seasonal changes in the milk or the conditions during production, and tasting the cheese allows you to be sure that you are buying it at its best.

In addition to this breadth of choice, a cheesemonger offers depth of knowledge. He or she can help you put together a cheeseboard or suggest which cheeses might best accompany the wine you have bought. Cheeses go through different stages of development, changing in both flavour and texture as they age. A young Stilton, for example, will be much firmer in texture and sharper in taste than an older one, where the texture has become creamy and the flavour richer and more mellow. Good cheesemongers can tell you which of their cheeses will be perfect that evening or at their best in a week's time, and it is always worth asking them for a recommendation. A helpful cheesemonger can make buying your cheese a pleasant journey of discovery, suggesting alternatives that you might not have come across before and helping you to try new varieties beyond your old favourites.

CARE AND QUALITY

Responsible cheesemongers go to a lot of trouble to ensure that the cheeses they stock are stored and cared for correctly. Cheeses are turned regularly to ensure that the moisture inside remains evenly distributed, and brushed or wiped down to ensure that no unwanted moulds develop that might affect the flavour. In short, behind the eye-catching display in a good cheesemonger's, much care goes into tending the cheeses to keep them at their best.

Some cheesemongers take looking after their cheese stock one stage further. They buy their farmhouse cheeses young from the cheesemakers, and manage their development themselves. This process – which in France is called *affinage* – involves bringing on the cheeses until the cheesemonger feels that they are at their optimum, for example, by controlling the temperature and humidity of the atmosphere in which the cheese is stored. A good maturer, or *affineur*, can make a real difference to the quality and flavour of the cheese, which is ideally then sold at its peak. To make the most of this expertise, always keep your cheeses wrapped separately in either clingfilm or waxed paper to prevent them drying out.

PERSONAL SERVICE

As well as recommending new cheeses to try, a good cheesemonger will cut you a small piece to try before you buy, and sell it at the size you require.

SERVING CHEESE

A SIMPLE RULE TO ENSURE THAT YOUR CHEESES taste their best is to bring them to room temperature before you eat them. Remove them from the fridge an hour before serving, keeping them wrapped until they reach the table. When offering cheese after a meal, one type at its best can be just as effective as a complicated selection. A splendid piece of fine Stilton or hand-made farmhouse Cheddar is a striking way to round off a meal.

Of course, if you want to make sure that you will be catering for all tastes, offer a selection. It is, however, still a good idea to limit the choice to three or four cheeses, so that they can be fully appreciated. A delicate fresh cheese, a pungent washed-rind, a favourite hard, and a tangy blue make up a classic selection. For additional variety, choose cheeses made from different milks: a soft goat's milk cheese, a hard sheep's milk cheese, and a blue cow's milk cheese, for example.

You will find that thin oatcakes, unflavoured wafer biscuits, or fresh bread make an excellent accompaniment, as they do not overpower the cheese, allowing its flavour to be fully appreciated. Cheese and fruit make a classic combination, with the sweetness of apples and grapes contrasting deliciously with the saltiness of cheese.

CHOOSING WINE

Choosing a wine to match your cheese is a complex business, not least because such a wide variety is available. Red wine is often thought to be the best accompaniment, but in fact many white wines complement cheese equally well. As a broad rule of thumb, serve lighter wines with more delicate cheeses; Sauvignon Blanc, for example, goes well with fresh or soft goat's cheeses. Similarly, match more strongly flavoured cheeses with a full-tasting wine; try serving a farmhouse Cheddar with a rich white wine or a washed-rind cheese with a Gewürztraminer. Steer clear of overly oaky wines, which are very hard to match successfully.

Port is the traditional accompaniment for blue cheeses such as Stilton, but it is also worth trying other dessert wines such as Sauternes, Monbazillac, or a sweet white wine. Bear in mind, as well, that many cheeses go well with other alcoholic drinks such as cider or beer.

There is no better way to finish a meal than with fine cheese, whether you serve a complementary selection of textures and flavours, or a single variety matured to perfection.

PERFECT COMBINATION
Cheese and wine make a classic pairing, especially after a meal. White wines go particularly well with many types, from soft goat's cheeses to tasty washed-rind cheeses.

FRESH CHEESES

These are the "babies" of the cheese world – young cheeses that are ready for selling in a matter of days from the milk's initial curdling. They are characterized by a lack of rind or mould, and a soft, moist delicate texture. Unless flavoured by the addition of herbs or garlic, fresh cheeses have a simple, fresh taste.

BLACK CROWDIE ROSS-SHIRE

Made by Highland Fine Cheeses in Tain, Scotland, this is a contemporary take on crowdie, a traditional Scottish cheese. Made from skimmed milk, with added double cream, the shaped cheese is rolled in pinhead oatmeal and crushed black peppercorns, and sold within a day or so. The textured brown-and-black coating gives the cheese a distinctive appearance and a pungent and peppery flavour.

SIZE	
D. 4cm (1½in)	
H. 8cm (3¼in)	
WEIGHT	
110g (3¾oz)	
SHAPE Log	
MILK Pasteurized	
RENNET None	
TYPE Traditional	

BOCADDON FARM CORNWALL

This fresh cheese made by Bocaddon Farm, near Looe, uses milk from the farm's herd of Guernsey cows. The curd is drained in muslin to remove the whey, then shaped, and is ready to eat in a week. At that stage it has a soft yellow paste and a creamy taste, with the richness of the Guernsey milk coming through. Flavoured versions include herb and garlic (shown here), black olive, and cracked black pepper.

SIZE	
D. 13cm (5in)	
H. 4cm (1½in)	
WEIGHT	
250g (9oz) or 500g (1lb 2oz)	
SHAPE Half-moon or round	
MILK Pasteurized cow's	
RENNET Vegetarian	
TYPE Modern	

CABOC ROSS-SHIRE

The richness of this cheese, produced by Highland Fine Cheeses in Tain, Scotland, is explained by the fact that it is made entirely from double cream, with a lactic starter used instead of rennet. The thickened cream is shaped into small logs and coated in golden brown oatmeal. The soft yellow paste inside has a buttery creaminess, which contrasts with the texture and nutty flavour of the oatmeal coating.

SIZE	
D. 4cm (1½in)	
L. 8cm (3¼in)	
WEIGHT	
110g (3¾oz)	
SHAPE Log	
MILK Pasteurized cow's double cream	
RENNET None	
TYPE Modern	

CERNEY PYRAMID
GLOUCESTERSHIRE

This goat's cheese is made by Cerney Cheese at Chapel Farm, near Cirencester. A fine black ash coating, using a mixture of oak ash and sea salt from France, gives it a striking appearance, with the black ash contrasting with the bright white paste. The texture is moist, and the cheese has a clean, sharp taste with a lemony freshness.

SIZE	
D. 6cm (2½in) base; 4cm (1½in) top	
H. 5cm (2in)	
WEIGHT	
250g (9oz)	
SHAPE Truncated pyramid	
MILK Unpasteurized goat's	
RENNET Vegetarian	
TYPE Fresh	

COWSLIP EAST SUSSEX

This small fresh cheese is made by High Weald Dairy using pasteurized organic milk from the dairy's own herd of cows. Just a touch of rennet is used to set the curd, which is then moulded into rounds. Ready for eating at just a few days, it is a creamy-coloured cheese with a soft, light texture and a mild flavour. It is also available in a version that is flavoured with chopped chives, shown here.

SIZE	
D. 6cm (2½in)	
H. 3cm (1¼in)	
WEIGHT	
100g (3½oz)	
SHAPE Round	
MILK Pasteurized organic cow's	
RENNET Vegetarian	
TYPE Modern	

CROWDIE AYRSHIRE

Made by Dunlop Dairy, this Scottish fresh cheese uses milk from the dairy's own herd of Ayrshire cows. Crowdie is a traditional Highlands' cheese, historically made from skimmed milk and eaten a day after making. Dunlop Dairy's crowdie is coated in oatmeal mixed with flecks of ground black pepper. The soft, moist white paste contrasts with the nuttiness and slight pepperiness of the coating.

SIZE	
D. 4cm (1½in)	
L. 8cm (3¼in)	
WEIGHT	
140g (5oz)	
SHAPE Log	
MILK Pasteurized cow's	
RENNET Vegetarian	
TYPE Traditional	

ELDREN DORSET

Named after a local wood, this fresh cheese is made by Cranborne Chase Cheese in Ashmore using unpasteurized cow's milk from a single herd at a local farm. The uncut curd is scooped into moulds and left to drain under its own weight for 48 hours. It is then hand-salted, chilled, and sold four days after making. The resulting cream-coloured cheese has a moist texture and a delicate lactic freshness.

SIZE	
D. 6cm (2½in) base; 5.5cm (2¼in) top	
H. 5.5cm (2¼in)	
WEIGHT	
175g (6oz)	
SHAPE Slightly tapering cylinder	
MILK Unpasteurized cow's	
RENNET Traditional animal	
TYPE Modern	

FAIRLIGHT EAST SUSSEX

This certified biodynamic, salt-free fresh cheese is made by Holly Park Organics using unpasteurized milk from its own free-range flock of goats, which are predominantly British Saanen. The morning milk is curdled using vegetarian rennet, hung initially in muslin, then drained under its own weight in moulds. Sold at a week old, it has a soft texture and a fresh, clean taste, with barely a hint of goat.

SIZE	
L. 7.5cm (3in)	
H. 4cm (1½in)	
WEIGHT	
200g (7oz)	
SHAPE Log	
MILK Unpasteurized biodynamic goat's	
RENNET Vegetarian	
TYPE Modern	

FINGALS CORNWALL

Menallack Farmhouse, near Penryn, makes this young cheese. Produced from Cornish goat's milk, the curd is moulded, unpressed (drained under its own weight), brine-bathed, and ready to eat within 24 hours. It has a moist white paste and a fresh lactic flavour. It is also made in a flavoured herbed version, in which the cheese is rolled in a mixture of finely chopped lemon grass, rosemary, and tarragon.

SIZE	
D. 6cm (2½in)	
H. 4cm (1½in)	
WEIGHT	
120g (4¼oz)	
SHAPE Round	
MILK Pasteurized goat's	
RENNET Vegetarian	
TYPE Modern	

HELIGAN CORNWALL

This large fresh cheese is made by Menallack Farmhouse, near Penryn, and is named after Cornwall's famous "Lost Gardens of Heligan". Unusually, it is made from a mixture of both sheep's and cow's milk. Unpressed, the cheese is ready to eat within 24 hours. Finely grated lemon zest is sprinkled over the cheese so that the soft, moist white paste has a citrus note, as well as an underlying milky mildness.

SIZE	
D.17cm (6¾in)	
H. 2cm (¾in)	
WEIGHT	
800g (1¾lb)	
SHAPE Square	
MILK Pasteurized sheep's and cow's	
RENNET Vegetarian	
TYPE Fresh	

INNES BUTTON **STAFFORDSHIRE**

This dainty little cheese is hand-made at the Highfields Dairy, Tamworth, using unpasteurized milk from the dairy's own herd. The fresh milk is used for cheese-making while still warm, which is key to its characteristic delicacy of texture. At five days, the tiny bright white cheese has an elegant, smooth texture like a firm mousse, and a fresh, salty taste. It is flavoured with a rosemary topping.

SIZE	
D. 5cm (2in)	
H. 2.5cm (1in)	
WEIGHT	
50g (1¾oz)	
SHAPE Button	
MILK Unpasteurized goat's	
RENNET Vegetarian	
TYPE Modern	

KNOCKALARA **WATERFORD**

Knockalara Farmhouse Cheese in Knockalara makes this Irish fresh cheese using pasteurized sheep's milk. The milk is curdled by the addition of vegetarian rennet, and the fragile curds are allowed to drain under their own weight. Ready to eat when only a few days old, the delicate white cheese has a soft, light texture and a fresh, clean flavour, with hardly a hint of sheep to it.

SIZE	
D. 30cm (12in)	
H. 8cm (3¼in)	
WEIGHT	
1.5kg (3lb 3oz)	
SHAPE Round	
MILK Pasteurized sheep's milk	
RENNET Vegetarian	
TYPE Modern	

MRS FINN CORNWALL

This fresh cheese, made by Menallack Farmhouse, near Penryn, is unusual because it is produced using a mixture of both sheep's and cow's pasteurized milk, as well as a lacing of single cream. The moulded curd drains under its own weight and is ready to eat within 24 hours. The resulting cheese has a moist white to cream-coloured paste and a simple, clean lactic taste.

SIZE	
D. 9cm (3½in)	
H. 3cm (1¼in)	
WEIGHT	
240g (8½oz)	
SHAPE Round	
MILK Pasteurized sheep's and cow's	
RENNET Vegetarian	
TYPE Modern	

NANTERROW CORNWALL

Menallack Farmhouse, near Penryn, makes this large fresh cheese, using pasteurized sheep's milk. The moist curds are moulded, left to drain under their own weight, and lightly salted. Ready to eat within 24 hours of making, the white paste is moist and spreadable, and has a simple lactic flavour. A herbed version (shown below) is also available, flavoured with chives, garlic, and black pepper.

SIZE	
D. 30cm (12in)	
H. 2.5cm (1in)	
WEIGHT	
2kg (4½lb)	
SHAPE Round	
MILK Pasteurized sheep's	
RENNET Vegetarian	
TYPE Modern	

OAKDOWN DEVON

This fresh goat's cheese is made at Oakdown Farm, Trusham, using unpasteurized milk from the farm's own herd of mixed goats. The moist curd is hung to drain, and the cheese is ready to eat within 48 hours of starting the making. It has a soft bright white paste and a gentle sweetness of flavour, and the version flavoured with garlic and herbs (shown below) has a flecked appearance.

SIZE	
D. 6cm (2½in)	
H. 5cm (2in)	
WEIGHT	
175g (6oz)	
SHAPE Round	
MILK Unpasteurized goat's	
RENNET Vegetarian	
TYPE Modern	

PANT YS GAWN GWENT

This small fresh Welsh goat's cheese is made by Abergavenny Fine Foods at Abergavenny. The organic goat's milk used to make the cheese is supplied by a number of farms from around Wales. It is a white round of cheese, without any rind or mould, with a light, moist yet crumbly curd and a clean, fresh flavour. There is a very faint and delicate lemon note to it.

SIZE	
D. 6cm (2½in)	
H. 3cm (1¼in)	
WEIGHT	
100g (3½oz)	
SHAPE Round	
MILK Pasteurized organic goat's milk	
RENNET Vegetarian	
TYPE Modern	

PERROCHE HEREFORDSHIRE

Made by Neal's Yard Creamery, this dainty rindless goat's cheese is eaten very fresh. Following a long coagulation, the curds are gently scooped into moulds and allowed to drain under their own weight. The resulting white cheese has a high moisture content, delicate texture, and a fresh, slightly tangy flavour with only a hint of goat. It is available plain or, as shown, rolled in rosemary, dill, or tarragon.

SIZE	
D. 6cm (2½in) base; 5cm (2in) top	
H. 7cm (2¾in)	
WEIGHT	
150g (5½oz)	
SHAPE Slightly tapering cylinder	
MILK Unpasteurized goat's	
RENNET Traditional animal	
TYPE Modern	

ROSARY WILTSHIRE

This fresh cheese is made by Chris and Claire Moody of Rosary Goats Cheese on their farm; they have been making goat's milk cheeses since 1986. Ready to eat at three days, Rosary has a moist bright white paste with a meltingly soft texture and a pleasantly sharp, salty taste with a subtle hint of goat. It is also available in flavoured versions, including garlic and pink peppercorns.

SIZE	
D. 5cm (2in)	
H. 4cm (1½in)	
WEIGHT	
100g (3½oz)	
SHAPE Round	
MILK Pasteurized goat's	
RENNET Vegetarian	
TYPE Modern	

GOAT'S MILK CHEESES
Appreciated for their flavour and digestibility, goat's milk cheeses have become increasingly popular and are now widely available.

STICHILL ROXBURGHSHIRE

This small fresh cheese is made by Brenda Leddy of Stichill Jerseys at Garden Cottage Farm, Kelso, using unpasteurized milk from the farm's own Jersey cows. The uncut curds are placed in muslin for two days, then salted and sold at a week old. The soft, pale yellow paste has a sweet creaminess to it. Flavoured versions are also made, including chives, herbs and garlic, black pepper (shown here), and sage and apple.

SIZE	
D. 5cm (2in)	
H. 2cm (¾in)	
WEIGHT	
85g (3oz)	
SHAPE Round	
MILK Unpasteurized cow's	
RENNET Vegetarian	
TYPE Modern	

SUSSEX SLIPCOTE WEST SUSSEX

Made from organic sheep's milk by High Weald Dairy, this is a light cheese with a fluffy texture, and is sold at three days old. The picturesque name is said to mean a "little piece" of cheese. The texture is soft and spreadable, and the cheese has a lactic, lemony fresh taste. The dairy produces the cheese plain and in a variety of flavoured versions, including garlic and herb (shown here), peppercorn, mint, and basil.

SIZE	
D. 5.5cm (2¼in)	
H. 4.5cm (1¾in)	
WEIGHT	
100g (3½oz)	
SHAPE Button	
MILK Pasteurized organic sheep's	
RENNET Vegetarian	
TYPE Modern	

VULSCOMBE DEVON

This delicate goat's cheese is hand-made by Graham and Josephine Townsend. The curd is created using the acid curd method, in which the milk's acidity is raised through using a starter and by being heated gently for a long time. The drained and salted curds are pressed for 24 hours. The resulting week-old cheese (available plain or flavoured) has a white paste with a soft texture and mild creamy flavour.

SIZE	
D. 7.5cm (3in)	
H. 4cm (1½in)	
WEIGHT	
175g (6oz)	
SHAPE Round	
MILK Pasteurized goat's	
RENNET None	
TYPE Modern	

WINDRUSH OXFORDSHIRE

Windrush Valley Goat Dairy in Windrush makes this small fresh cheese using milk from its own herd of Saanen goats. Both the milk and the fragile curd are carefully attended to by hand throughout the making process. Sold at five days old, Windrush has a creamy texture and fresh flavour, with only a very subtle hint of goat. It is also available flavoured with fresh herbs or crushed black peppercorns, as shown.

SIZE	
D. 6cm (2½in)	
H. 3cm (1¼in)	
WEIGHT	
115g (4oz)	
SHAPE Round	
MILK Pasteurized goat's	
RENNET Vegetarian	
TYPE Modern	

SOFT CHEESES

These young cheeses are ripened for only a few weeks, and are often made using goat's milk or sheep's milk. Soft-textured cheeses, which tend to be flat and thin, include white mould-ripened cheeses, with their characteristic white bloomy mould coating, and natural mould cheeses.

AIKET AYRSHIRE

This is a white mould-ripened cheese, made by Dunlop Dairy in Scotland, using milk from the dairy's own herd of Ayrshire cows. The moulded curd is drained under its own weight, given a brine bath, and ripened over four weeks. The resulting cheese has a white bloomy rind and a pale smooth paste which softens from the outside in. The flavour is salty with a very slight bitter note.

SIZE	
D. 9cm (3½in)	
H. 2cm (¾in)	
WEIGHT	
200–250g (7–9oz)	
SHAPE Round	
MILK Pasteurized cow's	
RENNET Vegetarian	
TYPE Modern	

BAKESEY MEADOW DEVON

Made for Country Cheeses by Debbie Mumford on the Sharpham Estate, this is a white mould-ripened cheese produced from unpasteurized goat's milk. Matured for four to six weeks, it has a coating of bloomy white mould over a glossy white paste, which softens from the outside in as the cheese ripens. The texture of the cheese is smooth and soft, and the flavour salty-sweet with a faint goaty note.

SIZE	
D. 7.5cm (3in) & 13cm (5in)	
H. 2.5cm (1in)	
WEIGHT	
200g (7oz) & 420g (15oz)	
SHAPE Round	
MILK Unpasteurized goat's	
RENNET Vegetarian	
TYPE Modern	

BATH SOFT CHEESE SOMERSET

Made by the Bath Soft Cheese Company at Park Farm, Kelston, this organic cheese
is produced using milk from the farm's own herd. Historically, Bath Cheese was a
traditional soft creamy cheese, the making of which was revived by the company
during the 1980s. The white bloomy rind contrasts with the smooth, glossy primrose
yellow paste, while the flavour is creamy and buttery with a full, salty mushroominess.

SIZE	
D. 10cm (4in)	
H. 3cm (1¼in)	
WEIGHT	
225g (8oz)	
SHAPE	Square
MILK	Pasteurized organic cow's
RENNET	Vegetarian
TYPE	Traditional

BLACK-EYED SUSAN SOMERSET

Made by Daisy & Co, this flavoured organic cheese is named after a flower of the daisy
family. The core cheese is a white mould-ripened cheese, made from locally sourced
organic Jersey cow's milk, lightly rolled in black peppercorns while young. Ready to eat
at three weeks, the cheese continues to ripen from the outside, becoming softer. The
smooth, creamy mild-tasting paste contrasts with the peppery exterior.

SIZE	
D. 10cm (4in)	
H. 2.5cm (1in)	
WEIGHT	
150g (5½oz)	
SHAPE	Round
MILK	Pasteurized organic cow's
RENNET	Vegetarian
TYPE	Modern

BUXLOW WONMIL SUFFOLK

Made by Margaret Reeves on her farm at Friston using milk from her own herd, this soft cheese is named after Buxlow, a lost Suffolk parish, with "wonmil" being a Suffolk dialect word for a full-fat cheese. Margaret gently cuts the delicate curd by hand, whereupon it is moulded and drained under its own weight. Sold within two days of making, it is a soft-textured white cheese with a fresh lactic flavour.

SIZE	
D. 25cm (10in)	
H. 2.5cm (1in)	
WEIGHT	
1.5kg (3lb 3oz)	
SHAPE Round	
MILK Pasteurized cow's	
RENNET Vegetarian	
TYPE Modern	

CAPRICORN GOAT SOMERSET

This small white mould-ripened goat's cheese is made by Lubborn Cheese at its creamery at Cricket Saint Thomas. The goat's milk is sourced from goat herds in Somerset and Dorset. The young moulded cheeses are dusted with salt and ripened for seven weeks, during which time they develop a fine white mould rind. The paste inside is a glossy white with a soft texture and a light, salty-sweet flavour.

SIZE	
D. 6cm (2½in)	
H. 4cm (1½in)	
WEIGHT	
120g (4¼oz)	
SHAPE Cylinder	
MILK Pasteurized goat's	
RENNET Vegetarian	
TYPE Modern	

CAWS PRESELI PEMBROKESHIRE

Pant Mawr in Wales makes this white mould-ripened cheese. *Penicillium candidum* is added to the milk with the starter at the beginning of the cheese-making process, and the cheese is matured for three weeks. The resulting Caws Preseli has a dusting of white mould bloom and a smooth ivory-coloured paste, dotted with a few holes. The flavour is mild and sweet, with a faintly bitter aftertaste.

SIZE	
D. 18cm (7in)	
H. 3cm (1¼in)	
WEIGHT	
900g–1.1kg (2–2½lb)	
SHAPE Round	
MILK Pasteurized cow's	
RENNET Vegetarian	
TYPE Modern	

CELESTE DEVON

This white mould-ripened cheese made for Country Cheeses by cheesemaker Debbie Mumford on the Sharpham Estate uses Jersey cow's milk. Matured for four to six weeks, Celeste has a bloomy white mould rind, contrasting with the smooth, glossy yellow paste. As it ripens, the paste softens from the outside in to an oozing consistency. The flavour is buttery with a mushroomy richness.

SIZE	
D. 15cm (6in)	
H. 2.5cm (1in)	
WEIGHT	
675g (1½lb)	
SHAPE Wheel	
MILK Unpasteurized cow's	
RENNET Vegetarian	
TYPE Modern	

CHABIS EAST SUSSEX

Made by Kevin and Alison Blunt on Greenacres Farm, this white mould-ripened cheese is based on a French goat's cheese, as its name suggests. It is made on the farm using unpasteurized milk from the Blunts' own herd of goats. An unpressed cheese, it is sold at around 12 days old. The thick white-mould rind coats a smooth ivory-coloured paste, while the flavour has a nutty quality.

SIZE	
D. 5cm (2in)	
H. 4cm (1½in)	
WEIGHT	
60g (2oz)	
SHAPE Cylinder	
MILK Unpasteurized goat's	
RENNET Vegetarian	
TYPE Modern	

CHATEL CORNWALL

This white mould-ripened cheese made by Cornish Country Larder at its creamery near Padstow uses full-fat cow's milk locally sourced from Pant Mawr in Wales, with added Cornish double cream. The cheese is ripened for 10 days, by the end of which it is covered in a layer of bloomy white mould and has a shiny ivory-coloured paste. As the cheese ripens, it softens from the outside in and has a mild, creamy flavour.

SIZE	
D. 9cm (3½in)	
H. 3cm (1¼in)	
WEIGHT	
200g (7oz)	
SHAPE Round	
MILK Pasteurized cow's	
RENNET Vegetarian	
TYPE Modern	

CHEMMY DEVON

This cheese's unusual name is in honour of the British downhill skier Chemmy Alcott. It is a white mould-ripened goat's cheese made for Country Cheeses by Debbie Mumford at the Sharpham Estate near Totnes. Matured for four to six weeks, it has a pale apricot-coloured rind, blotched with white mould, and a soft, light dryish paste, white in colour. The flavour is lactic and yoghurty, with lemony, goaty notes.

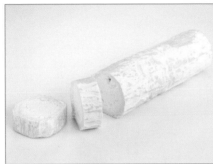

SIZE	
D. 5cm (2in)	
L. 18cm (7in)	
WEIGHT	
350g (12oz)	
SHAPE Log	
MILK Unpasteurized goat's	
RENNET Vegetarian	
TYPE Modern	

CLAVA INVERNESS

Connage Highland Dairy at Milton of Connage farm, Ardersier, makes this white mould-ripened cheese using organic milk from the farm's own mixed herd of Holstein–Friesians, Jersey crosses, and Norwegian Reds. The *Penicillium candidum* used to ripen the cheese is added to the milk with the starter. Sold at three weeks, the cheese has a white bloomy rind and a yellow paste with a mild flavour.

SIZE	
D. 11cm (4½in) & 25cm (10in)	
H. 3cm (1¼in)	
WEIGHT	
250g (9oz) & 1.5kg (3lb 3oz)	
SHAPE Round	
MILK Pasteurized organic cow's	
RENNET Vegetarian	
TYPE Modern	

COOLEENEY co TIPPERARY

Made by Cooleeney Cheese, Moyne, in Ireland, this is a white mould-ripened cheese that uses cow's milk from the farm's own herd of cows. Cooleeney is made using both vegetarian rennet and animal rennet, and pasteurized and unpasteurized milk. It is ripened for two months, during which time it develops a bloomy white rind over a pale yellow paste, which has an earthy, mushroomy flavour.

SIZE	
D. 7cm (2¾in)	
H. 2.5cm (1in)	
WEIGHT	
200g (7oz)	
SHAPE Round	
MILK Pasteurized & unpasteurized cow's	
RENNET Traditional animal & vegetarian	
TYPE Modern	

CRANNOG DUMFRIES

This young full-fat Scottish soft cheese is made from locally sourced unpasteurized cow's milk by the Loch Arthur Community Creamery in Beeswing, Dumfries. An unpressed cheese, it is sold at a week old, with its thin wax coating giving it a long shelf life. The white paste is soft and crumbly, and it has a melting texture and a mild lactic sourness. It is also available flavoured with herbs, chives, or green peppercorns.

SIZE	
D. 9cm (3½in)	
H. 3cm (1¼in)	
WEIGHT	
250g (9oz)	
SHAPE Round	
MILK Unpasteurized cow's	
RENNET Vegetarian	
TYPE Modern	

DORSTONE HEREFORDSHIRE

A soft goat's cheese made by Neal's Yard Creamery, Dorstone is named after the village in which the creamery is based. The curd is pre-drained which gives the cheese a distinctive light, fluffy texture. The cheese is coated in ash and matured for two weeks, allowing white, blue, and green moulds to develop, which contrast visually with the white paste inside. The texture is dryish, and it has a salty-sweet flavour.

SIZE	
D. 6cm (2½in)	
H. 8cm (3¼in)	
WEIGHT	
175g (6oz)	
SHAPE Cylinder	
MILK Unpasteurized goat's	
RENNET Traditional animal	
TYPE Modern	

ELMHIRST DEVON

A white mould-ripened triple-cream cheese made by Sharpham Creamery on the Sharpham Estate, Elmhirst uses unpasteurized milk from Jersey cows and double cream. Sold at four weeks, it has a white bloomy mould coating over an apricot-coloured rind with a primrose yellow paste. When young, the texture is firm and the flavour delicate; the cheese becomes meltingly soft with a rich flavour as it ripens.

SIZE	
D. 8cm (3¼in) & 15cm (6in)	
H. 5.5cm (2¼in)	
WEIGHT	
300g (10½oz) & 1kg (2¼lb)	
SHAPE Square & round	
MILK Unpasteurized cow's	
RENNET Vegetarian	
TYPE Modern	

FARLEIGH WALLOP SOMERSET

Made by Peter Humphries at White Lake Cheeses, Bagborough Farm, this white mould-ripened cheese is produced from goat's milk from the farm's own herd. The sprigs of thyme pressed into the white mould crust make the cheese easily recognizable. The smooth white paste softens with age, and the flavour is salty and mushroomy with a herbal note from the thyme.

SIZE	
D. 8cm (3¼in)	
H. 3cm (1¼in)	
WEIGHT	
115g (4oz)	
SHAPE Round	
MILK Thermized goat's	
RENNET Vegetarian	
TYPE Modern	

FINN HEREFORDSHIRE

Made by Neal's Yard Creamery, this cheese is produced from unpasteurized cow's milk with added double cream. A small amount of rennet is used to curdle the milk, and the curds have a long coagulation. Ready to eat at three weeks, the cheese has a white bloomy mould coating and a smooth primrose yellow paste. As the cheese ripens, the texture becomes luxuriously melting with a rich salty-sweet flavour.

SIZE	
D. 10cm (4in)	
H. 5cm (2in)	
WEIGHT	
300g (10½oz)	
SHAPE Round	
MILK Unpasteurized cow's	
RENNET Traditional animal	
TYPE Modern	

FLOWER MARIE EAST SUSSEX

A white mould-ripened cheese, Flower Marie is made from sheep's milk by Greenacres Farm, near Lewes. The recipe was developed by the Blunts together with pioneering cheesemaker James Aldridge. The gently handled curds drain under their own weight. The moulded cheeses are brined and matured, during which time they develop a white mould rind. The smooth ivory paste has a melting texture and subtle flavour.

SIZE	
D. 6cm (2½in) & 12cm (4¾in)	
H. 5cm (2in) & 4cm (1½in)	
WEIGHT	
200g (7oz) & 500–600g (1lb 2oz–1lb 5oz)	
SHAPE Square	
MILK Unpasteurized sheep's	
RENNET Vegetarian	
TYPE Modern	

GEVRIK CORNWALL

This white mould-ripened goat's cheese is made by Cornish Country Larder at its creamery at Trevarrian, near Padstow. The full-fat goat's milk used to make Gevrik is brought in from a number of farms around the country. The resulting cheese has a thin white mould rind over a smooth, glossy pale paste, which softens as the cheese ripens. The flavour is mild and fresh with a very slight goatiness.

SIZE	
D. 6cm (2½in)	
H. 4cm (1½in)	
WEIGHT	
75g (2½oz)	
SHAPE Round	
MILK Pasteurized goat's	
RENNET Vegetarian	
TYPE Modern	

GOLDEN CROSS EAST SUSSEX

This cheese is made by Greenacres Farm, near Lewes, using unpasteurized milk from the farm's goats. It is based on a French cheese, Saint Maure, and the milk undergoes a long coagulation, with the fragile curd gently handled throughout the making process. The cheese is coated in layer of ash, over which a white mould rind develops. The white paste has a fine, soft texture and a delicate flavour.

SIZE	
D. 5cm (2in)	
L. 14cm (5½in)	
WEIGHT	
250g (9oz)	
SHAPE Log	
MILK Unpasteurized goat's	
RENNET Vegetarian	
TYPE Modern	

GOAT'S MILK

British and Irish cheeses made from goat's milk were once a rarity, but today a wide range is produced. Goat's milk cheeses used to be regarded with caution, suspected of having an unpleasant "billy goat" taint to their flavour. These days, however, careful handling of the milk allows more delicate flavours to be appreciated.

Historically, goats were prized for their ability to thrive in barren terrain. Their lactation period is shorter than that of cows, and goat's milk cheeses were traditionally made between February and November. Bright white in colour, goat's milk has a higher fat content than cow's milk but the fat particles are far smaller, so that both the milk and the cheese are prized for their digestibility.

DAIRY GOATS
Although they can be reared in all climates, dairy goats should be kept in a dry, well-ventilated shelter.

GOLDILOCKS SOMERSET

A white mould-ripened cheese made from locally sourced organic Jersey cow's milk by Daisy & Co. In order to produce the white bloomy mould coating, *Penicillium candidum* is added to the milk along with a starter. The moulded cheeses are ripened and ready to eat at three weeks old. The even white mould rind coats a smooth, glossy pale yellow paste with a mild salty-sweet flavour with a hint of mushroom.

SIZE	
D. 10cm (4in)	
H. 2.5cm (1in)	
WEIGHT	
150g (5½oz)	
SHAPE Round	
MILK Pasteurized organic cow's	
RENNET Vegetarian	
TYPE Modern	

INDIAN BLANKET SOMERSET

Made by Daisy & Co, this smoked, white mould-ripened cheese is produced from locally sourced organic Jersey cow's milk. The brine-bathed, moulded young cheese is ripened, smoked very gently for eight hours, then ripened again. The resulting cheese, ready to eat at around three weeks, has a dry pale brown rind with white mould still visible, while the pale yellow paste has a subtle smoked flavour.

SIZE	
D. 10cm (4in)	
H. 2.5cm (1in)	
WEIGHT	
150g (5½oz)	
SHAPE Round	
MILK Pasteurized organic cow's	
RENNET Vegetarian	
TYPE Modern	

INNES ASH LOG STAFFORDSHIRE

Innes Cheese at Highfields Dairy of Tamworth makes this cheese using unpasteurized milk from its herd of goats. The curds are very carefully ladled into moulds, with the emphasis on handling them as lightly as possible to drain under their own weight. The black ash coating, in contrast to the white paste inside, makes it a striking-looking cheese. The texture is smooth, and it has a clean-tasting flavour with a lemony note.

SIZE
D. 5cm (2in)
L. 12cm (4¾in)
WEIGHT
150g (5½oz)
SHAPE Log
MILK Unpasteurized goat's
RENNET Vegetarian
TYPE Modern

INNES LEAF STAFFORDSHIRE

Attractively packaged with a chestnut leaf wrapped around it, this is a white mould-ripened cheese made by Innes Cheese at Highfields Farm Dairy. The unpasteurized milk comes from the dairy's herd of goats and is used for cheese-making while still warm. Aged for three weeks, the cheese has a bloomy white mould coating and a smooth gleaming white paste. The taste is salty-sweet with a faint goatiness.

SIZE
D. 10cm (4in)
H. 4cm (1½in)
WEIGHT
200g (7oz)
SHAPE Round
MILK Unpasteurized goat's
RENNET Vegetarian
TYPE Modern

ISLE OF WIGHT ISLE OF WIGHT

Made by Isle of Wight Cheese, this is a white mould-ripened cheese produced using unpasteurized Guernsey cow's milk from the dairy farm at which Isle of Wight Cheese is based. The cheese is sold at five weeks, by which time it has a bloomy white mould rind over a smooth yellow paste which continues to soften as it ripens. The flavour of the cheese is creamy with mushroomy notes.

SIZE	
D. 9cm (3½in)	
H. 3cm (1¼in)	
WEIGHT	
160g (5¾oz)	
SHAPE Round	
MILK Unpasteurized cow's	
RENNET Vegetarian	
TYPE Modern	

KELSEY LANE WEST MIDLANDS

This modern sheep's cheese is made by Berkswell Cheese at Ram Hall Farm using unpasteurized milk from the farm's own Friesland sheep. A white mould-ripened cheese, Kelsey Lane develops a bloomy white mould over a pale golden rind as it matures. The smooth-textured ivory-coloured paste has a mushroomy savouriness with a nutty sheep note to it. It is available in flavoured versions, as well as plain.

SIZE	
D. 8cm (3¼in)	
H. 3cm (1¼in)	
WEIGHT	
200g (7oz)	
SHAPE Wheel	
MILK Unpasteurized sheep's	
RENNET Vegetarian	
TYPE Modern	

KELSTON PARK SOMERSET

A white mould-ripened organic cheese made by the Bath Soft Cheese Company at Park Farm, Kelston, near Bath, Kelston Park uses milk from the farm's herd of Friesian cows and is named after the parkland where the cattle graze. The cheese has an even coating of bloomy white mould and a pale creamy yellow paste, which softens and darkens from the outside in as the cheese ripens. The flavour is mild and mushroomy.

SIZE	
D. 14cm (5½in)	
H. 4cm (1½in)	
WEIGHT	
675g (1½lb)	
SHAPE Round	
MILK Pasteurized organic cow's	
RENNET Vegetarian	
TYPE Modern	

KIDDERTON ASH CHESHIRE

Made by Ravens Oak Dairy at Nantwich, Chester, this is a white mould-ripened cheese produced from goat's milk supplied to the dairy. The young moulded cheeses are dipped first into brine, to add salt to the cheese, then into *Penicillium*, to create the white mould coating. The cheese is also coated in a fine layer of black food ash, through which the white mould grows; the dryish white paste has a mild flavour.

SIZE	
D. 4cm (1½in)	
L. 8cm (3¼in)	
WEIGHT	
150g (5½oz)	
SHAPE Log	
MILK Pasteurized goat's	
RENNET Vegetarian	
TYPE Modern	

LIGHTWOOD CHASER
GLOUCESTERSHIRE

Made by Lightwood Cheese, Chaser contains full-fat cow's milk and double cream. Sold at two to three weeks, it continues to ripen, reaching its peak at seven weeks. The white bloomy mould coats a pale cream-coloured paste with a melting texture. The mild, sweet flavour contrasts with the taste of the rind.

SIZE	
D. 7cm (2¾in)	
H. 2.5-3cm (1-1¼in)	
WEIGHT	
275g (9½oz)	
SHAPE Round	
MILK Unpasteurized cow's	
RENNET Vegetarian	
TYPE Modern	

LITTLE RYDING SOMERSET

Made by Wootton Organic at North Wootton, Little Ryding uses unpasteurized milk from the dairy's own flock of sheep. The recipe for the cheese was created by noted cheesemaker Mary Holbrook, who passed it on to Wootton Organic. It is a white mould-ripened cheese, with the orange-gold rind visible under the bloomy white coating. It has an ivory paste with a mushroomy salty-sweetness and a silky texture.

SIZE	
D. 10cm (4in)	
H. 3cm (1¼in)	
WEIGHT	
200g (7oz)	
SHAPE Round	
MILK Unpasteurized sheep's	
RENNET Vegetarian	
TYPE Modern	

LITTLE WALLOP SOMERSET

This striking-looking cheese is made for the Evenlode Partnership of Juliet Harbutt and Alex James by Peter Humphries of White Lake Cheese. The cheese is washed in Somerset Cider Brandy, then wrapped in vine leaves. It is ready to eat at three weeks when the brown rind has developed white and grey moulds. As it ripens, the smooth bright white paste softens, and the fresh, salty flavour develops a nutty complexity.

SIZE	
D. 8cm (3¼in)	
H. 4cm (1½in)	
WEIGHT	
115g (4oz)	
SHAPE Round	
MILK Thermized goat's	
RENNET Vegetarian	
TYPE Modern	

MAY HILL GREEN
GLOUCESTERSHIRE

Charles Martell at Hunts Court made this cheese and named it after a local landmark. It is easily identifiable due to the coating of chopped green nettles. Made from full-fat cow's milk, it has a glossy pale yellow paste which takes on a melting texture. The subtle iron flavour of the nettle coating contrasts with the soft, salty paste inside.

SIZE	
D. 13cm (5in) & 21cm (8¼in)	
H. 2.5cm (1in)	
WEIGHT	
500g (1lb 2oz) & 1.5kg (3lb 3oz)	
SHAPE Wheel	
MILK Pasteurized cow's	
RENNET Vegetarian	
TYPE Modern	

SOFT CHEESES

As white rind cheeses ripen, the bacteria in the mould work from the surface of the cheeses inwards, causing them to soften from the outside in.

MORNISH ISLE OF MULL

Isle of Mull Cheeses at Sgriob-ruadh Farm Dairy, Tobermory, on the Isle of Mull makes this white mould-ripened cheese, using milk from its own cows. *Penicillium candidum* is added to the milk to create the white bloomy mould coating on the cheese. It is sent out at three weeks, when it is young and firm. As it ripens, the pale yellow paste softens from the outside in. The flavour is mild and creamy.

SIZE	
D. 11cm (4½in) & 20cm (8in)	
H. 4cm (1½in)	
WEIGHT	
500g (1lb 2oz) & 1kg (2¼lb)	
SHAPE Round	
MILK Unpasteurized cow's	
RENNET Vegetarian	
TYPE Modern	

OLD BURFORD SOMERSET

Made by Wootton Organic on its farm and dairy at North Wootton, this mould-ripened cheese uses organic Jersey cow's milk supplied by a neighbour. Traces of the golden rind are visible under the white mould coating, while the paste is a primrose yellow, softening at the edges as the cheese ripens. The flavour, while reflecting the buttery creaminess of the Jersey milk, has a notable salty-sweetness.

SIZE	
D. 10cm (4in)	
H. 3cm (1¼in)	
WEIGHT	
220g (7¾oz)	
SHAPE Round	
MILK Unpasteurized cow's	
RENNET Vegetarian	
TYPE Modern	

PENYSTON GLOUCESTERSHIRE

This organic cheese is made by Daylesford Creamery using unpasteurized organic milk from the estate's herd of Friesians and traditional animal rennet. A mould-ripened cheese, it is rind-washed as it matures, and develops a bloomy white mould coating over an apricot-coloured rind. At four weeks, the yellow paste has a chalky texture and a clean, lemony flavour; at six weeks, the texure is voluptuous and the flavour buttery.

SIZE	
D. 3cm (1¼in)	
H. 10cm (4in)	
WEIGHT	
300g (10½oz)	
SHAPE Square	
MILK Unpasteurized cow's	
RENNET Traditional animal	
TYPE Modern	

PERL WEN DYFED

This organic white mould-ripened cheese is made by Caws Cenarth in Wales. The bloomy white mould rind covers a pale yellow paste, which, as is characteristic of this type of cheese, softens from the outside in. As the cheese ripens, it also develops in flavour. When young, the flavour is very mild and faintly lemony; as it matures, it becomes richer and sweeter with a salty aftertaste.

SIZE	
D. 20cm (8in)	
H. 3cm (1¼in)	
WEIGHT	
2kg (4½lb)	
SHAPE Round	
MILK Pasteurized organic cow's	
RENNET Vegetarian	
TYPE Modern	

PONT GAR WHITE
CARMARTHENSHIRE

This white mould-ripened cheese is made by the Carmarthenshire Cheese Company. The name comes from "Sir Gar", Welsh for Carmarthenshire. It has a thick, even coating of white mould over a smooth, sticky pale yellow paste. As it ripens, the paste softens from the outside. A mild, creamy cheese, it has a faint mushroomy note.

SIZE	
D. 11cm (4½in)	
H. 4cm (1½in)	
WEIGHT	
250g (9oz)	
SHAPE Round	
MILK Pasteurized cow's	
RENNET Vegetarian	
TYPE Modern	

RAGSTONE HEREFORDSHIRE

This soft log-shaped goat's cheese is made by Neal's Yard Creamery. When Charlie Westhead started making the cheese, Neal's Yard Creamery was based in Kent, and its name derives from the Ragstone Ridge there. The cheese is moulded in pipes, which give it a characteristic log shape, and has a white bloomy rind and smooth white paste. It has a smooth lactic flavour and is excellent grilled.

SIZE	
H. 5cm (2in)	
L. 15cm (6in)	
WEIGHT	
300g (10½oz)	
SHAPE Log	
MILK Pasteurized cow's	
RENNET Vegetarian	
TYPE Modern	

SHARPHAM DEVON

Made since 1980 by Sharpham Creamery on the Sharpham Estate near Totnes, using unpasteurized milk from the estate's own Jersey cows, this is a white mould-ripened cheese. Sharpham is ready to eat at four weeks, by which time it is coated in a bloomy white mould over a smooth yellow paste which is firm when young, softening as it ripens. The flavour is mild and creamy when young, and stronger when ripe.

SIZE	
D. 9.5cm (3¾in) & 19cm (7¼in)	
H. 4cm (1½in) & 4.5cm (1¾in)	
WEIGHT	
250g–1 kg (9oz–2¼lb)	
SHAPE Square & round	
MILK Unpasteurized cow's	
RENNET Vegetarian	
TYPE Modern	

SHEPHERD'S CROOK SOMERSET

As its name suggests, this is a sheep's milk cheese, made by Wootton Organics, North Wootton, using unpasteurized milk from its own flock of sheep. Ready to eat at three to four weeks, this is a mould-ripened cheese with a golden rind blotched with a fine coating of bloomy white mould and a glossy white paste, which softens from the outside in as the cheese ripens. The flavour is clean and fresh.

SIZE	
D. 9cm (3½in)	
H. 5cm (2in)	
WEIGHT	
220g (7¾oz)	
SHAPE Round	
MILK Pasteurized cow's	
RENNET Vegetarian	
TYPE Modern	

SLEIGHTLETT SOMERSET

This small, delicate goat's milk cheese is hand-made by Mary Holbrook at Sleight Farm, near Timsbury, Bath. Only a little rennet is used to curdle the milk, so the curd is fragile and requires careful handling. The distinctive black ash coating, sometimes mottled with blue and green moulds, covers a brilliant white cheese. The flavour is refreshingly clean and lactic, with a hint of goat; the texture is smooth and velvety.

SIZE	
D. 7.5cm (3in)	
H. 3–4cm (1¼–1½in)	
WEIGHT	
200g (7oz)	
SHAPE Wheel	
MILK Unpasteurized goat's	
RENNET Traditional animal	
TYPE Modern	

ST EADBURGHA WORCESTERSHIRE

A white mould-ripened cheese made by Gorsehill Abbey Farm, this cheese uses milk from the farm's herd. A *Penicillium* mould is sprayed onto the cheeses, which are then matured and eaten at 4–12 weeks, depending on their size. By this stage, the white mould has grown over the apricot-coloured rind, while the ivory paste inside is smooth and shiny. Creamy-textured, it softens as it ripens, and has a full, mushroomy flavour.

SIZE	
D. 9–35cm (3½–13¾in)	
H. 4cm (1½in)	
WEIGHT	
175g–3kg (6oz–6½lb)	
SHAPE Round	
MILK Pasteurized cow's	
RENNET Traditional animal	
TYPE Modern	

ST GEORGE EAST SUSSEX

Nut Knowle Farm at Horam makes this white mould-ripened goat's cheese using full-fat milk from its own herd of goats. The bloomy white mould grows over a pale yellow rind, while the paste is pale cream in colour. St George is sold at two weeks, when it is a firm young cheese with only a mild hint of goat. As the cheese ages and ripens, it softens from the outside in and develops in flavour.

SIZE	
D. 10cm (4in)	
H. 3cm (1¼in)	
WEIGHT	
280g (10oz)	
SHAPE Round	
MILK Pasteurized goat's	
RENNET Vegetarian	
TYPE Modern	

ST KEVERNE CORNWALL

Made by the Lambrick family at Toppenrose Dairy, this white mould-ripened cheese uses milk from their Friesian herd. The name is inspired by the nearby village of St Keverne, visible from the farm, which does indeed have a square. Sold at three to four weeks, the cheese develops a white mould rind over a pale yellow paste, which softens as the cheese ripens. It tastes mild and mellow, with mushroomy overtones.

SIZE	
D. 9.5cm (3¾in)	
H. 2.5cm (1in)	
WEIGHT	
250g (9oz)	
SHAPE Square	
MILK Pasteurized cow's	
RENNET Vegetarian	
TYPE Modern	

ST KILLIAN CO WEXFORD

Carrigbyrne Farmhouse Cheese in Ireland makes this white mould-ripened cheese, named after a Wexford saint, using milk from the farm's own herd of Friesians. *Penicillium candidum* is added to the milk at the start of the cheese-making, and it is sold at 12 days old when it has a bloomy white rind and a pale yellow paste. As the cheese ripens it softens, developing a melting texture, and it has a milky, mild flavour.

SIZE	
D. 7cm (2¾in) & 10cm (4in)	
H. 2.5cm (1in)	
WEIGHT	
150g (5½oz) & 250g (9oz)	
SHAPE Round & hexagonal	
MILK Pasteurized cow's	
RENNET Vegetarian	
TYPE Modern	

ST TOLA CO CLARE

This soft organic goat's cheese is made by Inagh Farmhouse Cheese, Ireland, using unpasteurized milk from the farm's own goats. As it matures, St Tola develops a distinctively whorled pale gold rind, from the *Geotrichum* mould, over the soft bright white paste. At its best at four weeks, the cheese has a melting texture and a sweet fullness of flavour with a faint, lingering fresh tang of goat.

SIZE	
D. 7.5cm (3in)	
L. 25cm (10in)	
WEIGHT	
1kg (2¼lb)	
SHAPE Log	
MILK Unpasteurized organic goat's	
RENNET Traditional animal	
TYPE Modern	

TOPPENROSE GOLD CORNWALL

Toppenrose Dairy at Trenance makes this little soft cheese using milk from its own herd of Friesian cows. Locally sourced Jersey double cream is added to the milk, resulting in a white mould-ripened cheese with a noticeably golden yellow paste. The cheese is sold at five to six weeks, by which time the smooth paste has softened to a creamy texture, and the cheese has a rich creaminess of flavour.

SIZE	
D. 6cm (2½in)	
H. 5cm (2in)	
WEIGHT	
100g (3½oz)	
SHAPE Round	
MILK Pasteurized cow's	
RENNET Vegetarian	
TYPE Modern	

RENNET

Curdling the milk to separate solid fat and protein from the liquid is an essential part of the cheese-making process. This is most commonly achieved using rennet, a substance containing the enzyme rennin (also known as chymosin). The traditional source of rennet was the lining of the fourth stomach of a calf or other young dairy animal. This lining was salted and dried to preserve its properties, and cut into strips that were added to vats of soured milk to trigger the curdling. Today, animal rennet is available to cheesemakers in liquid or powder form.

Cheesemakers can also use vegetarian alternatives. Plants such as lady's bedstraw (*Galium verum*) or the wild cardoon (*Cynara cardunculus*) have been used in the past to curdle milk, but modern cheesemakers tend to rely on rennet produced from the fungus *Mucor miehei* or the bacterium *Bacillus subtilis*. It is also possible to manufacture chymosin in the laboratory using genetic engineering techniques, creating a substance identical to animal rennet without using calf cells.

TRICKLE SOMERSET

This dainty cheese is one of a range of goat's milk cheeses made by Peter Humphries of White Lake Cheeses at Bagborough Farm, using unpasteurized milk from the farm's herd of Saanen, Toggenberg, British Alpine, and Anglo-Nubian goats. A white mould-ripened cheese, it has an even coating of bloomy white mould over its rind and a smooth white paste. The flavour is mild and sweet with a goaty tang.

SIZE	
D. 5.5cm (2¼in)	
H. 2cm (¾in)	
WEIGHT	
50g (1¾oz)	
SHAPE Round	
MILK Unpasteurized goat's	
RENNET Vegetarian	
TYPE Modern	

TUNWORTH HAMPSHIRE

Similar in style to a French Camembert, Tunworth is a modern cheese hand-made on a family farm in Hampshire by Julia Cheyney and Stacey Hedges of Hampshire Cheese, using milk from a local herd of Holstein cattle. The resulting cheese, with its wrinkled white rind is eaten at between four to six weeks, and has a soft, creamy texture. The flavour is mellow and nutty with mushroomy notes.

SIZE	
D. 11cm (4½in)	
H. 3cm (1¼in)	
WEIGHT	
250g (9oz)	
SHAPE Disc	
MILK Unpasteurized cow's	
RENNET Traditional animal	
TYPE Modern	

TYMSBORO SOMERSET

The natural rind of this goat's cheese varies in appearance, coated predominantly with either white mould or green and blue over a fine coating of black ash. It is hand-made by Mary Holbrook at Sleight Farm, near Timsbury, Bath, using milk from her own goats. The texture of the paste ranges from creamy soft near the edge to smooth and firm at the centre, while the flavour is rich with a subtle tang.

SIZE	
D. 8cm (3¼in) base; 4cm (1½in) top	
H. 7.5cm (3in)	
WEIGHT	
250g (9oz)	
SHAPE Truncated pyramid	
MILK Unpasteurized goat's	
RENNET Traditional animal	
TYPE Modern	

VIPERS GRASS SOMERSET

Strikingly named, this flavoured organic cheese is made by Daisy & Co in Somerset. It is a white mould-ripened cheese made from organic Jersey cow's milk, sourced locally. The chopped chives and garlic are added to the milk at the beginning of the cheese-making process. A dainty sprinkling of chives marks the bloomy white mould rind. The pale yellow paste is smooth in texture and has a subtle savoury flavour.

SIZE	
D. 10cm (4in)	
H. 2.5cm (1in)	
WEIGHT	
150g (5½oz)	
SHAPE Round	
MILK Pasteurized organic cow's	
RENNET Vegetarian	
TYPE Modern	

WATERLOO BERKSHIRE

Village Maid Cheese makes this at its creamery near Reading using unpasteurized milk from Guernsey cows. The curd is washed, removing some of the acidity, and the moulded cheese is brined. Ripened for 4–10 weeks, Waterloo develops a white rind, dusted with mould, and a soft yellow paste. The flavour is mild and creamy when young, and richer and fuller as the cheese ripens and the texture softens.

SIZE	
D. 16cm (6½in)	
H. 4.5cm (1¾in)	
WEIGHT	
675g (1½lb)	
SHAPE Round	
MILK Unpasteurized cow's	
RENNET Vegetarian	
TYPE Modern	

WEALDEN EAST SUSSEX

This small goat's cheese is made by Nut Knowle Farm at Horam using pasteurized full-fat milk from the farm's own flock of British Toggenburg and Saanen goats. When young, the cheese has an ivory-coloured rind over a white paste which has a mild, sweet flavour with a goaty tang. As the cheese ages, it darkens in colour and takes on a stronger, much more goaty flavour.

SIZE	
D. 5cm (2in)	
H. 5cm (2in)	
WEIGHT	
80g (2¾oz)	
SHAPE Round	
MILK Pasteurized goat's	
RENNET Vegetarian	
TYPE Modern	

WEALDWAY EAST SUSSEX

Nut Knowle Dairy at Nut Knowle Farm, Horam, makes this cheese using full-fat goat's milk from the farm's own herd of Toggenburg and Saanen goats. The curds are ladled into moulds and drained under their own weight. The cheese is a smooth bright white log with a soft but dryish paste with a delicate, slightly goaty flavour. It is also available in flavoured versions, coated in herbs or seeds.

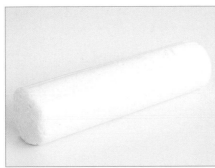

SIZE	
D. 5.5cm (2¼in)	
L. 14cm (5½in)	
WEIGHT	
150g (5½oz)	
SHAPE Log	
MILK Pasteurized goat's	
RENNET Vegetarian	
TYPE Modern	

WHITE HEART SOMERSET

This romantic-shaped white mould-ripened soft cheese is made by White Lake Cheeses at Bagborough Farm using milk from its goats. At the start of the cheese-making, the milk is thermized (that is, heated for at least 15 seconds at a temperature between 57°C/135°F and 68°C/154°F). Ready to eat at three to four weeks, it has a white bloomy covering over a soft, moist white paste and a very fresh delicate flavour.

SIZE	
D. 8cm (3¼in)	
H. 4cm (1½in)	
WEIGHT	
200g (7oz)	
SHAPE Heart	
MILK Thermized goat's	
RENNET Vegetarian	
TYPE Modern	

WHITE LAKE SOMERSET

White Lake Cheeses at Bagborough Farm makes this white mould-ripened cheese using milk from the farm's own herd of Saanen, Toggenburg, British Alpine, and Anglo-Nubian goats. The cheese is matured for between four to six weeks, during which time it develops a fine bloomy white rind over the interior paste, which is smooth and ivory-coloured. The flavour is clean with a hint of goat and a long finish.

SIZE	
D. 10cm (4in)	
H. 2.5cm (1in)	
WEIGHT	
210g (7½oz)	
SHAPE Round	
MILK Thermized goat's	
RENNET Vegetarian	
TYPE Modern	

SHEEP'S MILK

Sheep's milk was always the most widely used milk in British cheese-making – it was used, for example, to make Wensleydale (see page 182). As cows, with their high milk yield, became the favoured dairy animal, fewer cheeses were made from sheep's milk. Today, however, there has been a revival, with a number of British cheesemakers producing sheep's milk cheese.

Sheep's milk has appreciably more solids in it than either cow's or goat's milk, and is high in fats and protein, allowing for a high yield of cheese from the milk. Sheep's milk is naturally homogenized with the very small-sized fat molecules in the milk remaining evenly mixed throughout, making it easily digestible. Bright white in colour, it has a rich, nutty flavour which characterizes many sheep's milk cheeses.

DAIRY SHEEP
Sheep's milk was used in early cheese-making, but sheep were also valued for their meat and wool.

WHITEHAVEN CHESHIRE

Made by the Ravens Oak Dairy at Nantwich, this is a white mould-ripened cheese produced from locally sourced goat's milk. The moulded curd is dipped first into brine, to add salt to the cheese, then in a *Penicillium* mould, which creates the dense coating of bloomy white mould over the cheese. The paste inside is white and smooth, firm when young and softening as it ripens, and the cheese has a mildly goaty flavour.

SIZE	
D. 7.5cm (3in)	
H. 4cm (1½in)	
WEIGHT	
150g (5½oz)	
SHAPE Round	
MILK Pasteurized goat's	
RENNET Vegetarian	
TYPE Modern	

WITHYBROOK DEVON

This goat's cheese is made for Country Cheeses by Debbie Mumford on the Sharpham Estate. The moulded cheese is coated with black ash, a process particularly associated with goat's cheeses. Matured for four to six weeks, when it is ripened the cheese has a bloomy white mould covering a fine layer of black ash, with a gleaming white interior paste. This striking-looking sliced cheese has a dryish texture and a strong goaty tang.

SIZE	
D. 9cm (3½in) base; 5cm (2in) top	
H. 7.5cm (3in)	
WEIGHT	
300g (10½oz)	
SHAPE Truncated pyramid	
MILK Unpasteurized goat's	
RENNET Vegetarian	
TYPE Modern	

SEMI-SOFT CHEESES

With a slightly firmer texture than soft cheese, the semi-soft variety is, to put it bluntly, the smelliest group of cheeses. Washed-rind cheeses are easily identifiable by their powerful odour, sticky orange exteriors, and full-flavoured paste. Washed-curd cheeses, with their supple-textured paste, also fall into this group.

ADMIRAL COLLINGWOOD
NORTHUMBERLAND

Named after a Northumbrian naval hero, this washed-rind cheese from Doddington Dairy uses unpasteurized milk from the farm's cows. It is moulded and washed in Newcastle Brown Ale as it matures, and it develops an orange rind over a smooth yellow paste. The flavour is full and mellow with a distinctive lingering ale aftertaste.

SIZE	
D. 14cm (5½in) & 18cm (7in)	
H. 4cm (1½in)	
WEIGHT	
1kg (2¼lb) & 2kg (4½lb)	
SHAPE Square	
MILK Unpasteurized cow's	
RENNET Traditional animal	
TYPE Modern	

ADRAHAN CO CORK

Adrahan Farmhouse Cheese in Ireland makes this cheese, using pasteurized milk from the farm's own cows. During cheese-making, the rind is washed with brine. Matured for four to eight weeks, Adrahan develops a sticky, ridged golden-orange rind over a pale yellow paste, dotted with a few holes and a savoury aroma. The paste has a creamy, giving texture, and the flavour is mild yet complex.

SIZE	
D. 19.5cm (7½in)	
H. 5cm (2in)	
WEIGHT	
1.5kg (3lb 3oz)	
SHAPE Round	
MILK Pasteurized cow's	
RENNET Vegetarian	
TYPE Modern	

BISHOP KENNEDY **ARGYLL**

One of the few Scottish washed-rind cheeses, this is made by the Inverloch Cheese Company in Campbeltown. The curd is moulded but not pressed, then brined and washed with a solution containing *Brevibacterium linens* as it matures. Matured for three months, the cheese develops a sticky orange rind over a pale yellow paste. The texture is soft and smooth, and the flavour mild with a spicy note.

SIZE	
D. 23cm (9in)	
H. 4cm (1½in)	
WEIGHT	
1.7kg (3¾lb)	
SHAPE	Round
MILK	Pasteurized cow's
RENNET	Vegetarian
TYPE	Modern

BURWASH ROSE **EAST SUSSEX**

A washed-rind cheese made by the Traditional Cheese Dairy, Wadhurst, this cheese uses local unpasteurized cow's milk. A solution of *Brevibacterium linens* is added to the milk, and the cheese is matured for six to eight weeks, during which time it is washed with a brine solution containing rosewater. The resulting cheese has a ridged natural rind over a pale yellow paste with a moist texture and a mild, rich flavour.

SIZE	
D. 14cm (5½in)	
H. 6cm (2½in)	
WEIGHT	
800g (1¾lb)	
SHAPE	Round
MILK	Unpasteurized cow's
RENNET	Vegetarian
TYPE	Modern

CARK CUMBRIA

Martin Gott makes this cheese seasonally, during March to October, at Holker Farm Dairy using unpasteurized milk from the farm's goats. During the cheese-making, the rind of the cheese is washed, giving it the the orange-brown rind that is characteristic of washed-rind cheeses. The paste inside is white, with a moist, crumbly texture and a salty flavour that has an element of goat to it.

SIZE	
D. 20cm (8in)	
H. 10cm (4in)	
WEIGHT	
3kg (6½lb)	
SHAPE	Round
MILK	Unpasteurized goat's
RENNET	Traditional animal
TYPE	Modern

CAWS CERWYN PEMBROKESHIRE

Pant Mawr makes this unpressed cheese using cow's milk from the local co-operative. The curd is scalded, drained, moulded, and salted, then matured unwrapped for three weeks. At this stage, the cheese has a pale apricot-coloured rind, ridged from the mats on which it was drained, and is lightly dusted with white mould. The paste within is pale yellow with a moist texture and a mild, salty-sweet flavour.

SIZE	
D. 17cm (6¾in)	
H. 5cm (2in)	
WEIGHT	
1.2kg (2¾lb)	
SHAPE	Round
MILK	Pasteurized cow's
RENNET	Vegetarian
TYPE	Modern

CELTIC PROMISE CEREDIGION

Made by John Savage of Teifi Farmhouse Cheese using raw cow's milk sourced from a single herd, this shaped cheese is matured for seven weeks in a humid atmosphere. During this time it is washed twice a week with a solution containing *Brevibacterium linens*, which acts on the cheese to create flavour and texture. It has a sticky orange rind, a pungent smell, a soft, giving texture, and a rich, full flavour.

SIZE	
D. 7cm (2¾in)	
H. 5cm (2in)	
WEIGHT	
500g–600g (1lb 2oz–1lb 5oz)	
SHAPE Round	
MILK Unpasteurized cow's	
RENNET Vegetarian	
TYPE Modern	

BUFFALO'S MILK

It may come as a surprise to discover that there is a handful of cheesemakers in Britain today creating buffalo's milk cheeses. The water buffalo, with its placid temperament, has long been valued for its milk in countries including Italy (famous for its buffalo mozzarella), India, and Pakistan.

Very low in carotene, buffalo's milk is a pure brilliant white and is naturally homogenous, with the small fat globules evenly distributed. Buffalo's milk contains 58 per cent more calcium, 40 per cent more protein, and higher levels of lactose than cow's milk, and some believe because of its greater concentration of solids, it is far more digestible. More curd can be obtained from buffalo's milk, hence making more cheese than the equivalent amount of cow's milk.

HEALTHY CHOICE
Buffalo's milk contains around 40 per cent less cholesterol than cow's milk.

CRIFFEL DUMFRIES

This organic Scottish cheese is made by the Loch Arthur Community at Beeswing using milk from its biodynamic farm. Criffel is both a washed-curd and a washed-rind cheese, sprayed with a bacterial mixture containing *Brevibacterium linens* while it is ripened for a month. The cheese has a textured golden-orange rind and a smooth, shiny primrose yellow paste. Very flavoursome, it is sweet with pleasant bitter notes.

SIZE	
D. 18cm (7in)	
H. 4cm (1½in)	
WEIGHT	
1.8kg (4lb)	
SHAPE Square	
MILK Unpasteurized organic cow's	
RENNET Vegetarian	
TYPE Modern	

CROFTON CUMBRIA

Thornby Moor Dairy, Thursby, makes this cheese – one of the few cheeses produced from a mixture of milks – using both locally sourced cow's milk and goat's milk. Matured for at least two weeks at the dairy, the cheese develops a natural rind over a pale paste. The texture is soft and moist, while the flavour of the cow's milk comes through first, followed by an aftertaste from the goat's milk.

SIZE	
D. 14cm (5½in)	
H. 4cm (1½ in)	
WEIGHT	
500g (1lb 2oz)	
SHAPE Domed round	
MILK Unpasteurized cow's and goat's	
RENNET Vegetarian	
TYPE Modern	

DODDINGTON BALTIC
NORTHUMBERLAND

This washed-rind cheese from Doddington Dairy uses unpasteurized milk from the farm's cows and traditional animal rennet. Once moulded, the cheese is washed with Baltic Summer ale as it matures. It has a strong aroma, a golden-orange rind over a shiny pale yellow paste, and a long-lasting flavour with a sweet alcoholic note.

SIZE	
D. 18cm (7in)	
H. 4cm (1½in)	
WEIGHT	
1.8kg (4lb)	
SHAPE Round	
MILK Unpasteurized cow's	
RENNET Traditional animal	
TYPE Modern	

DRAGON'S BACK POWYS

Named after a peak in the Black Mountains, this Welsh cheese is made by Caws Mynydd Dhu on its farm at Brecon using sheep's milk from the farm's own Poll Dorset crosses. The curd is delicately handled during the making process, which involves milling and pressing. Matured for eight weeks in the cellar, it develops a pale natural rind and a creamy-textured paste that has a subtle flavour.

SIZE	
D. 11cm (4½in)	
H. 10cm (4in)	
WEIGHT	
900g (2lb)	
SHAPE Round	
MILK Pasteurized sheep's	
RENNET Vegetarian	
TYPE Modern	

DREWI SANT PEMBROKESHIRE

This small cheese is made by Pant Mawr using cow's milk brought in from a local co-operative. *Penicillium candidum* is added to the milk with the starter and the moulded, unpressed curd is sprayed with honey mead before being wrapped and left to mature. The cheese is ready for eating at three weeks, by which time it has a faint dusting of white mould and a soft, pale yellow paste with a full flavour.

SIZE	
D. 10cm (4in)	
H. 5cm (2in)	
WEIGHT	
900g–1.1kg (2lb–2½lb)	
SHAPE Round	
MILK Pasteurized cow's	
RENNET Vegetarian	
TYPE Modern	

DURRUS CO CORK

This Irish cheese has been made by Durrus Farmhouse Cheese since 1979. The unpasteurized cow's milk is sourced locally and curdled with traditional animal rennet. A washed-rind cheese, it develops an orange-pink rind over a yellow paste; the small cheeses are matured for two weeks, and the large for four to five weeks. When young, the flavour is mild; as it matures, it becomes more complex with a fruity, nutty taste.

SIZE	
D. 10cm (4in) & 18cm (7in)	
H. 5cm (2in) & 6cm (2½in)	
WEIGHT	
380g (13oz) & 1.5kg (3lb 3oz)	
SHAPE Round	
MILK Unpasteurized cow's	
RENNET Traditional animal	
TYPE Modern	

GUBBEEN CO CORK

Gubeen Farmhouse has been making this cheese since 1979 using milk from its cows. The moulded cheese is washed with white wine as it matures, to encourage the growth of the unique bacteria in the dairy that give the cheese its particular flavour. Matured for between three weeks to six months, depending on size, the cheese has a pink-orange rind over a smooth yellow paste with a creamy, mushroomy flavour.

SIZE
D. 10–30cm (4–12in)
H. 5–10cm (2–4in)
WEIGHT
500g–4kg (1lb 2oz–9lb)
SHAPE Round
MILK Pasteurized cow's
RENNET Vegetarian
TYPE Modern

IAMBORS SOMERSET

One of a handful of British buffalo's milk cheeses, this is made by Alham Wood Cheese in Shepton Mallet using organic milk from its own herd of buffalos. It is named after the Alham Wood's first buffalo bull. Iambors is covered with a coat of pale yellow wax, which protects the interior white paste. The texture is soft and crumbly, and the cheese has a mild lactic flavour.

SIZE
D. 18cm (7in)
H. 6cm (2½in)
WEIGHT
1.5–2kg (3lb 3oz–4½lb)
SHAPE Round
MILK Pasteurized buffalo's
RENNET Vegetarian
TYPE Modern

IONA CROMAG ISLE OF MULL

Isle of Mull Cheeses at Sgriob-ruadh Farm Dairy, Tobermory, makes this cheese using unpasteurized sheep's milk. As the cheese matures, it is rind-washed with Iona whisky from the Tobermory distillery and a solution containing *Brevibacterium linens*. Ready to eat at a month, Iona Cromag has a sticky pale orange rind and a moist light-coloured paste with a delicate buttery, mushroomy flavour.

SIZE	
D. 11cm (4½in) & 23cm (9in)	
H. 4cm (1½in)	
WEIGHT	
500g (1lb 2oz) & 2.5kg (5½ lb)	
SHAPE Round	
MILK Unpasteurized sheep's	
RENNET Vegetarian	
TYPE Modern	

KEBBUCK DUMFRIES

This distinctive-looking semi-soft cheese is made by the Loch Arthur Community at Beeswing using organic milk from its herd of cows. The curd is washed at a high temperature, a fact reflected in the cheese's supple texture, and hung in a cloth to mature for two months. It has a ridged dark brown rind and a pale yellow paste with a rich salty-sweet fullness of flavour that lingers.

SIZE	
D. 12cm (4¾in)	
H. 6cm (2½in)	
WEIGHT	
675–800g (1½–1¾lb)	
SHAPE Varies	
MILK Unpasteurized cow's	
RENNET Vegetarian	
TYPE Modern	

KELTIC GOLD CORNWALL

This semi-soft cheese is made by Whalesborough Farm Foods in Bude. During the making process the curd is washed, creating a particular supple texture. While the moulded cheese is maturing, it is washed with local cider. It is ready to eat at six weeks, by which time it has a sticky apricot-coloured rind and shiny, moist pale yellow paste with a pungent smell. The taste is creamy and full.

SIZE	
D. 20cm (8in)	
H. 7.5cm (3in)	
WEIGHT	
1.5kg (3lb 3oz)	
SHAPE Round	
MILK Pasteurized cow's	
RENNET Vegetarian	
TYPE Modern	

KILLIECHRONAN ISLE OF MULL

This sheep's milk cheese is made by Isle of Mull Cheeses at Sgriob-ruadh Farm Dairy, Tobermory, using unpasteurized milk. During the making process, the curd is washed, brined, and pressed into a basket which gives the cheese its distinctive form. Matured for six months, it is an ivory-coloured cheese with a moist, tender texture and a delicate flavour that has a long-lasting finish.

SIZE	
D. 6cm (2½in) & 7.5cm (3in)	
H. 16cm (6½in) & 23cm (9in)	
WEIGHT	
1.5kg (3lb 3oz) & 3kg (6½lb)	
SHAPE Oval	
MILK Unpasteurized sheep's	
RENNET Vegetarian	
TYPE Modern	

KNOCKDRINNA CO KILKENNY

This sheep's milk cheese is made by Knockdrinna Farmhouse Cheese, Stoneyford. The curd is washed, and while the cheese is matured for at least two months the rind is washed with organic white wine, during which time it takes on a deep pink-orange colour. The creamy-coloured paste, dotted with a few holes, has a supple texture, while the flavour is sweet and nutty with a long-lasting finish.

SIZE	
D. 23cm (9in)	
H. 8cm (3¼in)	
WEIGHT	
2.5kg (5½lb)	
SHAPE Round	
MILK Pasteurized sheep's	
RENNET Vegetarian	
TYPE Modern	

LAVISTOWN CO KILKENNY

Originally made by Olivia Goodwillie, a pioneer of the revival of Irish farmhouse cheese-making, Lavistown is now made by Knockdrinna Farmhouse Cheese. Using semi-skimmed milk, it is moulded and pressed, with the rind washed in the early stages, and brushed as it matures. Ready to eat at four weeks, it has a moist yellow paste and fresh, creamy flavour. As it matures, it becomes drier and stronger-tasting.

SIZE	
D. 23cm (9in)	
H. 9cm (3½in)	
WEIGHT	
3.5kg (7½lb)	
SHAPE Round	
MILK Pasteurized cow's	
RENNET Vegetarian	
TYPE Modern	

LITTLE STINKY CORNWALL

This irreverently named washed-rind cheese is made for Country Cheeses by Sue Proudfoot at Whalesborough Farm near Bude. Using pasteurized cow's milk, it is washed with a brine and mould solution as it matures. Ready to eat at two to three months, it has a sticky orange-coloured rind, while the paste is yellow with an almost meaty texture. As the name suggests, it has a distinctive smell and a mild, full flavour.

SIZE
D. 9cm (3½in)
H. 5cm (2in)
WEIGHT
400g (14oz)
SHAPE Round
MILK Pasteurized cow's
RENNET Vegetarian
TYPE Modern

MILLEENS CO CORK

The Steeles have been making Milleens on the Beare Peninsula in the south-west of Ireland since 1976. Using pasteurized milk from a neighbouring herd and animal rennet, this is a washed-rind cheese. The humid air in this part of Ireland encourages the growth of the moulds, and the maturing process sees an orange-pink rind develop over a yellow paste which has a rich, complex flavour and creamy texture.

SIZE
D. 10cm (4in) & 20cm (8in)
H. 3cm (1¼in) & 4cm (1½in)
WEIGHT
225g (8oz) & 1.3kg (3lb)
SHAPE Round
MILK Pasteurized cow's
RENNET Traditional animal
TYPE Modern

MISS MUFFET CORNWALL

Whalesborough Farm Foods, near Bude, makes this cow's milk semi-soft cheese. The curd is washed during the making process, giving it a supple texture. As the cheese matures, it develops a natural brown rind, which is flecked with white and pink mould. The resulting paste is smooth and pale yellow, and dotted with a few holes. The flavour is mild with a little zing at the end.

SIZE	
D. 7.5cm (3in) & 20cm (8in)	
H. 5cm (2in) & 10cm (4in)	
WEIGHT	
350g (12oz) & 1.5kg (3lb 3oz)	
SHAPE Round	
MILK Pasteurized cow's	
RENNET Vegetarian	
TYPE Modern	

MORN DEW SOMERSET

This cow's milk cheese is made at White Lake Cheeses, Bagborough Farm. During making the curd is washed, creating a supple texture, and the rind is washed as the cheese matures, being ready to eat at between six to seven weeks. By this stage Morn Dew has developed a sticky, thick orange-brown rind, while the paste is smooth and ivory-coloured. The flavour is full with a sweet nuttiness and a slight tang.

SIZE	
D. 18cm (7in)	
H. 6cm (2½in)	
WEIGHT	
1.8kg (4lb)	
SHAPE Round	
MILK Pasteurized cow's	
RENNET Vegetarian	
TYPE Modern	

OXFORD ISIS OXFORDSHIRE

This small washed-rind cheese is made for the Oxford Cheese Company, which sells cheese in Oxford. During its maturation, the cow's milk cheese is washed with honey mead, affecting both its texture and its flavour. When Oxford Isis is ready to eat, it has a strong penetrating odour, a sticky pale orange rind, and a pale yellow paste with a supple, giving texture and a full, mushroomy flavour.

SIZE	
D. 10cm (4in)	
H. 2.5cm (1in)	
WEIGHT	
225g (8oz)	
SHAPE	Round
MILK	Pasteurized cow's
RENNET	Vegetarian
TYPE	Modern

POLMESK CORNWALL

Menallack Farm at Treverna, near Penryn, makes this goat's cheese using Cornish goat's milk. The curd is moulded, brined, allowed to dry, then, when it is around a week old, waxed to preserve the cheese. The resulting cheese has a dark green wax coating, while the paste inside is bright white. The texture is at once firm and moist, while the flavour is very mild, only slightly salty, and with the merest hint of goatiness.

SIZE	
D. 17cm (6¾in)	
H. 7.5cm (3in)	
WEIGHT	
500g (1lb 2oz)	
SHAPE	Round
MILK	Pasteurized goat's
RENNET	Vegetarian
TYPE	Modern

POSBURY DEVON

This flavoured goat's cheese is made by Norworthy Dairy, Crediton, using unpasteurized milk from its herd of Saanen, Toggenburg, and British Alpine goats. It is a washed-curd cheese, flavoured with garlic, onion, horseradish, and paprika, and aged for a month. It has an orange rind over a springy white paste, dotted with holes and orange-red flecks. The flavour is mild with a faint spiciness to it.

SIZE	
D. 18cm (7in)	
H. 11cm (4½in)	
WEIGHT	
2–2.5kg (4½–5½lb)	
SHAPE Round	
MILK Pasteurized goat's	
RENNET Vegetarian	
TYPE Modern	

PUDDLE SOMERSET

This is made by White Lake Cheeses at Bagborough Farm using thermized milk (that is, heated for at least 15 seconds at a temperature between 57°C/135°F and 68°C/154°F) from the farm's own goats. A mould-ripened cheese, it is aged for around six weeks, and develops a pale brown rind blotched with grey and white mould. The white paste has a smooth texture, while its flavour is sweet and nutty.

SIZE	
D. 11cm (4½in)	
H. 2cm (¾in)	
WEIGHT	
100–140g (3½–5oz)	
SHAPE Round	
MILK Thermized goat's	
RENNET Vegetarian	
TYPE Modern	

WASHED RINDS

Many semi-soft varieties, such as Celtic Promise (see page 79), are washed with a bacterial solution as they mature in order to create a sticky orange rind.

RACHEL SOMERSET

White Lake Cheeses at Bagborough Farm makes this cheese using milk from its own goats. The curd is washed, creating a supple texture, and the rind is also washed as the cheese matures, being ready to eat at between six to seven weeks. By this stage the cheese has developed a sticky chestnut-coloured rind and a smooth white paste. The flavour is mild with a nutty, subtle goatiness to it.

SIZE	
D. 18cm (7in)	
H. 7cm (2¾in)	
WEIGHT	
2kg (4½lb)	
SHAPE	Round
MILK	Thermized goat's
RENNET	Vegetarian
TYPE	Modern

RUBY GOLD YORKSHIRE

Cheesemongers Cryer & Stott have created this novelty cheese, inspired by the local Wakefield rhubarb triangle. A young, moist sheep's milk cheese is halved and layered with salted rhubarb, then matured for seven days. The cheese is sold at two weeks old and has a moist white paste, with a visible layer running through it. The clean, fresh flavour of the cheese contrasts with the sweetness of the rhubarb.

SIZE	
D. 6cm (2½in)	
H. 3cm (1¼in)	
WEIGHT	
800g (1¾lb)	
SHAPE	Round
MILK	Pasteurized sheep's
RENNET	Vegetarian
TYPE	Modern

SAVAL CEREDIGION

Made by Teifi Farmhouse Cheese, using raw milk sourced from a single herd, this shaped cheese is matured for seven to eight weeks in a humid atmosphere. During maturing it is washed twice a week with a solution containing *Brevibacterium linens* that acts on the cheese to create flavour and texture. The resulting cheese has a sticky orange rind, a pungent smell, a soft, moist texture, and a rich, full flavour.

SIZE	
D. 26cm (10½in)	
H. 5cm (2in)	
WEIGHT	
2kg (4½lb)	
SHAPE Round	
MILK Unpasteurized cow's	
RENNET Vegetarian	
TYPE Modern	

SHARPHAM RUSTIC DEVON

This semi-soft cheese is made on the Sharpham Estate using unpasteurized milk from its Jersey cows. Unpressed, it is shaped in a colander and matured for six to eight weeks, during which time a pale natural rind, coated in white mould, forms over a rich yellow paste. The texture is creamy with a mild sweetness of flavour. Sharpham Rustic is also available flavoured with chives and garlic.

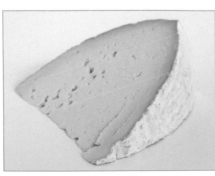

SIZE	
D. 18cm (7in)	
H. 9cm (3½in)	
WEIGHT	
1.7kg (3¾lb)	
SHAPE Oval	
MILK Unpasteurized cow's	
RENNET Vegetarian	
TYPE Modern	

SLOE TAVEY SOMERSET

Easy to spot due to its distinctive romantic shape, this heart-shaped goat's milk cheese is made for Country Cheeses by cheesemaker Peter Humphries of White Lake Cheeses. During maturation, the cheese is washed with Plymouth sloe gin to add flavour. Matured for two to three months, Sloe Tavey has a sticky orange-red rind and a powerful, penetrating odour with a rich, full flavour to match.

SIZE	
D. 9cm (3½in)	
H. 2.5cm (1in)	
WEIGHT	
300g (10½oz)	
SHAPE Heart	
MILK Unpasteurized goat's	
RENNET Vegetarian	
TYPE Modern	

ST GILES EAST SUSSEX

High Weald Dairy at Tremains Farm makes this semi-soft organic cheese using milk from the farm's herd of cows and naming it after the local Norman church. The inspiration was the Port Salut style of cheese found in France. The cheese's distinctive orange rind gains its colour from organic carrot juice. The pale yellow paste has a soft, moist texture, while the flavour is mild and creamy.

SIZE	
D. 24cm (9½in)	
H. 7–8cm (2¾–3¼in)	
WEIGHT	
2.7kg (6lb)	
SHAPE Round	
MILK Pasteurized organic cow's	
RENNET Vegetarian	
TYPE Modern	

ST JAMES CUMBRIA

Martin Gott makes this cheese at Holker Farm Dairy using unpasteurized milk from his own Lacaune sheep, and animal rennet. It is named in tribute to the late pioneering cheesemaker and maturer James Aldridge, who taught Martin how to make cheese. St James is washed with a brine solution as it matures, and has an orange rind over a firm, moist white paste with a nutty, salty flavour.

SIZE	
D. 20cm (8in)	
H. 4.5cm (1¾in)	
WEIGHT	
1.8kg (4lb)	
SHAPE Round	
MILK Unpasteurized sheep's	
RENNET Traditional animal	
TYPE Modern	

ST OSWALD WORCESTERSHIRE

This small organic cheese, named after a Worcestershire patron saint, is made by Gorsehill Abbey Farm using milk from its own herd of cows. A washed-rind cheese, it is matured for between one to three months, during which time the rind changes in colour from yellow to a rich orange. The smooth pale yellow paste has a rich fullness of flavour and a long-lasting finish.

SIZE	
D. 11cm (4½in) & 35cm (13¾in)	
H. 4.5cm (1¾in)	
WEIGHT	
350g (12oz) & 2.5kg (5½lb)	
SHAPE Round	
MILK Pasteurized organic cow's	
RENNET Traditional animal	
TYPE Modern	

STINKING BISHOP
GLOUCESTERSHIRE

Created and made by Charles Martell at Hunts Court, the inspiration for this cheese comes from the Cistercian monks who once farmed locally. As it matures, the rind is washed with perry (it is named after a perry pear variety). With a textured golden-orange rind and smooth yellow paste, it has a powerful odour and rich, savoury flavour.

SIZE	
D. 13cm (5in) & 21cm (8¼in)	
H. 4.5cm (1¾in) & 5cm (2in)	
WEIGHT	
500g (1lb 2oz) & 1.5kg (3lb 3oz)	
SHAPE Round	
MILK Pasteurized cow's	
RENNET Vegetarian	
TYPE Modern	

SUFFOLK GOLD SUFFOLK

Suffolk Farmhouse Cheeses near Cobham makes this cheese using the golden creamy milk from its herd of pedigree Guernsey cows. Lightly pressed, the cheese is matured for 10 weeks, developing a golden natural rind. The rich yellow paste is dotted with a few small holes and has a creamy texture and a mild sweetness of flavour, with the butteriness of the Guernsey cow's milk coming through.

SIZE	
D. 20cm (8in)	
H. 5cm (2in)	
WEIGHT	
3kg (6½lb)	
SHAPE Round	
MILK Pasteurized cow's	
RENNET Vegetarian	
TYPE Modern	

WHITE NANCY **SOMERSET**

This is a white mould-ripened semi-soft cheese, which is made by White Lake Cheeses at Bagborough Farm using milk from the farm's own herd of goats. The milk is thermized (that is, heated for at least 15 seconds at a temperature between 57°C/135°F and 68°C/154°F) at the start of the cheese-making process. The resulting cheese has a moist, crumbly paste and a delicate lactic flavour.

SIZE	
D. 11cm (4½in)	
H. 7cm (2¾in)	
WEIGHT	
500g (1lb 2oz)	
SHAPE Round	
MILK Thermized goat's	
RENNET Vegetarian	
TYPE Modern	

WIGMORE **BERKSHIRE**

The Wigmores of Village Maid Cheese make their eponymous cheese at their creamery. The sheep's milk is thermized and *Penicillium candidum* added to it while the curd is washed during the making process. As the cheese matures for between four to six weeks, it develops a coating of bloomy white mould over a pale paste inside. The soft paste has a creamy texture and a mild, nutty sweetness.

SIZE	
D. 10cm (4in) & 17cm (6¾in)	
H. 4cm (1½in)	
WEIGHT	
400g (14oz) & 800g (1¾lb)	
SHAPE Round	
MILK Unpasteurized sheep's	
RENNET Vegetarian	
TYPE Modern	

HARD CHEESES

These firm-textured cheeses are usually large and are matured
for several months. As ever with cheeses, diversity is the norm, and
hard cheeses have a notable range of textures, from the exquisite
crumbliness of a Kirkham's Lancashire to the dry firmness
of cheeses such as Montgomery's Cheddar or Gabriel.

ALLERDALE CUMBRIA

This hard goat's cheese was the first to be made by Thornby Moor Dairy, Crofton Hall, Thursby, and it still makes it today. A hard-pressed cheese, Allerdale is matured for at least six weeks, developing a natural rind, although it is best eaten at between three to four months old. When young, the pale paste has a moist, crumbly texture and a sweet, nutty flavour; when older, the paste is drier and the flavour more complex.

SIZE	
D. 10cm (4in) & 14cm (5½in)	
H. 10cm (4in) & 14cm (5½in)	
WEIGHT	
1kg (2¼lb) & 2.5kg (5½lb)	
SHAPE Truckle	
MILK Unpasteurized goat's	
RENNET Vegetarian	
TYPE Modern	

ASHDOWN FORESTERS
EAST SUSSEX

Named after Ashdown Forest in Sussex, this is made by High Weald Dairy at Tremains Farm using organic milk from its cows. The cheese is unpressed, taking its shape and textured golden natural rind from the basket in which it is formed. Matured for three months, it has a moist pale yellow paste and mild, nutty sweetness of flavour.

SIZE	
D. 22cm (8½in)	
H. 7–8cm (2¾–3¼in)	
WEIGHT	
2.2kg (5lb)	
SHAPE Basket	
MILK Pasteurized organic cow's	
RENNET Vegetarian	
TYPE Modern	

BELSTONE DEVON

Curworthy Cheese at Stockbeare Farm, Okehampton, makes this cheese using milk from its own herd of Friesian cows, and vegetarian rennet. The curd is cut, scalded, moulded, and pressed, with the cheese then matured for at least three months, developing a natural rind dusted with white mould. The paste is a pale yellow colour with a firm, smooth texture and a mild yet lingering flavour.

SIZE	
D. 14cm (5½in) & 18cm (7in)	
H. 6cm (2½in) & 9cm(3½in)	
WEIGHT	
1kg (2¼lb) & 2.5kg (5½lb)	
SHAPE Round	
MILK Pasteurized cow's	
RENNET Vegetarian	
TYPE Modern	

BELTANE CEREDIGION

This Welsh sheep's cheese made by Caws Celtica uses unpasteurized milk sourced from the maker's own flock of Friesland sheep. It is a curd-washed cheese, based on a Gouda recipe, in which the washed curds are moulded and matured from 3–18 months, depending on size. Once matured, the cheese has a white, mould-dusted golden-brown natural rind and a dryish pale paste with a lingering nutty sweetness.

SIZE	
D. 8–25cm (3¼–10in)	
H. 6–9cm (2½–3½in)	
WEIGHT	
250g–4.5kg (9oz–10lb)	
SHAPE Round & wheel	
MILK Unpasteurized sheep's	
RENNET Vegetarian	
TYPE Modern	

BERKSWELL WEST MIDLANDS

Named after the village in which it is made, this hard cheese is made by the Berskwell Cheese Company at Ram Hall using milk from its own sheep. Matured for around four months, the cheese develops a hard golden-orange rind, marked from the mould in which it was formed and blotched with mould. The cream-coloured paste inside has a hard, dense texture with a full, complex sweet nuttiness to its flavour.

SIZE	
D. 20cm (8in)	
H. 9cm (3½in)	
WEIGHT	
2.4kg (5¼lb)	
SHAPE Flattened sphere	
MILK Unpasteurized sheep's	
RENNET Traditional animal & vegetarian	
TYPE Modern	

BERWICK EDGE NORTHUMBERLAND

This large hard cheese is made by Doddington Dairy, North Doddington Farm, Wooler, using unpasteurized milk from the farm's own herd of cows. Matured for around 10 months, it is a Gouda-style cheese, developing a brown rind over a shiny rich yellow paste dotted with a few small holes. Berwick Edge has a powerful, sweet flavour that lingers on in the mouth.

SIZE	
D. 23cm (9in) & 32cm (12½in)	
H. 7cm (2¾) & 10cm (4in)	
WEIGHT	
5kg (11lb) & 10kg (22lb)	
SHAPE Round	
MILK Unpasteurized cow's	
RENNET Traditional animal	
TYPE Modern	

MATURING CHEESES

Some of the best cheesemongers mature young cheeses themselves. This is known as *affinage* in France, where the practice is more common.

BIRDOSWALD CUMBRIA

Named after a nearby Roman fort on Hadrian's Wall, this organic cheese is made by
Slack House Organic Farm. It is made to a Scottish Dunlop recipe, dating back to
1688, using milk from the farm's Ayrshire cows. The cheese is pressed, clothbound,
and matured for up to six months, developing a golden rind, dusted with mould, over
a rich yellow paste. The texture is firm and creamy, and the flavour is full.

SIZE	
D. 25cm (10in)	
H. 10cm (4in)	
WEIGHT	
9kg (20lb)	
SHAPE Cylinder	
MILK Unpasteurized organic cow's	
RENNET Vegetarian	
TYPE Modern	

BLARLIATH ROSS-SHIRE

This Scottish hard cheese is named after the farm in Tain where it is made by
Highland Fine Cheeses. The curd is "Cheddared" during the making process and the
moulded cheese double-wrapped in cloth and larded to keep the moisture in during
the nine months' maturing time. As it matures, Blarliath develops a pale natural rind
over a moist yellow paste which has a mild flavour.

SIZE	
D. 30cm (12in)	
H. 46cm (18in)	
WEIGHT	
18–22kg (40–48½lb)	
SHAPE Truckle	
MILK Pasteurized cow's	
RENNET Traditional animal	
TYPE Modern	

BUTTERCUP EAST SUSSEX

The Traditional Cheese Dairy in Wadhurst makes this cow's cheese using unpasteurized Jersey cow's milk, sourced from local dairies. The moulded cheese is matured for three to four months, during which time it develops a ridged brown natural rind, dotted with white mould over a paste which is a rich yellow colour, due to the Jersey cow's milk. The paste is firm and smooth, and the flavour mild and creamy.

SIZE	
D. 18cm (7in)	
H. 9cm (3½in)	
WEIGHT	
3.5kg (7½lb)	
SHAPE Cylinder	
MILK Unpasteurized cow's	
RENNET Vegetarian	
TYPE Modern	

BUXLOW PAIGLE SUFFOLK

Farmhouse Fayre, Friston, makes this cheese using milk from its herd of Friesians. The picturesque name "paigle" is from the Suffolk dialect name for a cowslip. To make the cheese, the curd undergoes a process of cutting, salting, and pressing in moulds. The moulded cheese is waxed and matured for two months. Under the dark green wax coating, the pale yellow paste is moist with a mild lactic flavour.

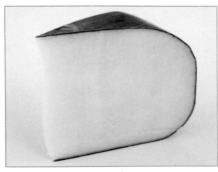

SIZE	
D. 30cm (12in)	
H. 12cm (4¾in)	
WEIGHT	
5kg (11lb)	
SHAPE Round	
MILK Pasteurized cow's	
RENNET Vegetarian	
TYPE Modern	

CAERPHILLY

DYFED, CEREDIGION, & SOMERSET

A TRADITIONAL WELSH CHEESE, Caerphilly takes its name from
the town and county in South Wales where it was first made.
Like other hard cheeses, it was valued as an easily portable,
nourishing food, and by 1830 demand was such that a cheese market had been set
up to cater for it. It was said to be a favourite with Welsh coal miners, as its shallow
depth and thick rind made it easy to eat with dirty hands, while its moist, salty paste
helped replace the minerals and moisture lost by the miners through sweat.

CHANGING TIMES

The 19th century saw demand for Caerphilly exceed supply. The coming of the
railways led many Welsh farmers to export their milk for sale rather than use it to
make Caerphilly. To fill the gap, Somerset farmers, who traditionally made slow-
maturing Cheddar, began making their own Caerphilly cheese. During World War II,
the making of Caerphilly was banned by the Ministry of Food in favour of longer-
lasting hard cheeses. Even after the war, when the restriction had been lifted, very
little Caerphilly was made in Wales other than in large-scale creameries. Farmhouse
production, however, was continued in Somerset, notably by Duckett's Caerphilly
(see overleaf), and recent years have seen a revival in farmhouse Caerphilly.

Made from cow's milk, farmhouse Caerphilly is wheel-shaped, only lightly
pressed to retain moisture in the curd, and eaten young. A classic Caerphilly such as
Gorwydd has a pale paste with a noticeably flaky texture and a fresh, lemony flavour.

GORWYDD
CAERPHILLY

SIZE	
D. 17cm (6¾in) & 25cm (10in)	
H. 7cm (2¾in) & 8cm (3¼in)	
WEIGHT	
2kg (4½lb) & 3.5–4kg (7½–9lb)	
SHAPE Round	
MILK Unpasteurized cow's	
RENNET Traditional animal	
TYPE Traditional	

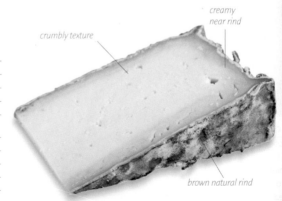

creamy near rind

crumbly texture

brown natural rind

GORWYDD CAERPHILLY

Gorwydd is made by the Trethowans in Ceredigion in the traditional way, using unpasteurized milk and animal rennet. Matured for two months, it has a brown natural rind and a pale yellow paste. Creamy near the rind and crumbly in the middle, the cheese has a fresh and lemony flavour.

CAWS CENARTH CAERPHILLY
DYFED

This organic Caerphilly is made by Caws Cenarth, using milk sourced from Ffosyficer Organic Farm, Pembrokeshire. The curd is cut, moulded, brined to seal the cheese, and lightly pressed, then matured for four to five weeks, at which time it is a pale yellow cheese with a flaky, moist texture. It has a fresh lactic flavour with a touch of citrus.

SIZE	
D. 25cm (10in)	
H. 8cm (3¼in)	
WEIGHT	
4kg (9lb)	
SHAPE Round	
MILK Pasteurized organic cow's	
RENNET Vegetarian	
TYPE Traditional	

DUCKETT'S CAERPHILLY
SOMERSET

Duckett's has been making Caerphilly since 1928. It uses unpasteurized milk from the dairy's herd, animal rennet, and traditional pint starters. The curd is pressed briefly, salted, pressed, brined, and matured for seven weeks. It develops a textured brown rind over a primrose-coloured paste with an open texture and a clean, citrussy flavour.

SIZE	
D. 25cm (10in)	
H. 7.5cm (3in)	
WEIGHT	
4kg (9lb)	
SHAPE Round	
MILK Unpasteurized cow's	
RENNET Traditional animal	
TYPE Traditional	

CAIRNSMORE DUMFRIES

This hard sheep's cheese is made by Galloway Farmhouse Cheeses in Sorbie using organic unpasteurized milk from the farm's own flock of sheep. The salted curd is pressed into moulds, then halved, wrapped, and stored, maturing for six months. The resulting matured cheese has an ivory-coloured paste with a smooth, dense texture and an initial sharp, salty flavour, which turns into a sweet sheepiness.

SIZE	
D. 18cm (7in)	
H. 23cm (9in)	
WEIGHT	
4kg (9lb)	
SHAPE Truckle	
MILK Unpasteurized sheep's	
RENNET Vegetarian	
TYPE Modern	

CAMPSCOTT DEVON

This organic cheese, made on Middle Campscott Farm, Ilfracombe, uses milk from the farm's sheep. Campscott is matured for two months, during which time it develops a grey-brown natural rind over a firm pale primrose yellow paste. The texture and flavour are creamier and sheepier when made in the winter, and drier and nuttier when made in the summer. It is also available flavoured with cumin seeds.

SIZE	
D. 10.5cm (4¼in) & 14cm (5½in)	
H. 10cm (4in) & 15cm (6in)	
WEIGHT	
1 kg (2¼lb) & 2kg (4½lb)	
SHAPE Cylinder	
MILK Pasteurized organic sheep's	
RENNET Vegetarian	
TYPE Modern	

CAMPSCOTT GOAT DEVON

Campscott Farm, Ifracombe, makes this organic hard cheese using unpasteurized milk from its own goats. The delicate curds are lightly pressed to mould them, then the shaped cheese is brined and matured for one month. This pale cheese has a fresh, barely goaty flavour when it is made in the winter, and a drier paste with a subtle taste of goat when it is made in the summer.

SIZE	
D. 14cm (5½in) & 13cm (5in)	
H. 9.5cm (3¾in) & 13cm (5in)	
WEIGHT	
960g (2lb 2oz) & 1.9kg (4¼lb)	
SHAPE Cylinder	
MILK Unpasteurized organic goat's	
RENNET Vegetarian	
TYPE Modern	

COW'S MILK

Britain's best-known traditional cheeses – Cheddar, Stilton, and Cheshire – are all made from cow's milk. Cows have a long lactation period, and their rich, creamy milk, which has large fat globules that rise to the surface and a firm casein structure, lends itself to cheese-making.

The most common breed in Britain's dairy industry is the black-and-white Friesian–Holstein, popular because of its high milk yield. Other breeds valued by cheesemakers include the Scottish Ayrshire, the rare Gloucester, and the Jersey. The milk varies from breed to breed, but is also affected by what the cows eat, the season, and the stage of lactation. Summer milk, produced when the cows have grazed on lush, rich pastures, rather than silage, is particularly valued by cheesemakers.

JERSEY COWS
The milk from Jersey cows is noted for its rich golden-yellow colour.

CAWS NANTYBWLA
CARMARTHENSHIRE

Caws Nantybwla makes this cheese to an old family recipe on its own farm using milk from its herd of pedigree Holsteins and Jerseys. It is a pressed cheese, matured for at least a month. It has a golden rind over a rich yellow paste. The texture is firm yet moist, and the flavour is full and tangy. This cheese is available in flavoured versions.

SIZE	
D. 7.5cm (3in) & 9cm (3½in)	
H. 7.5cm (3in) & 23cm (9in)	
WEIGHT	
2kg (4½lb) & 4½kg (10lb)	
SHAPE Round	
MILK Pasteurized & unpasteurized cow's	
RENNET Vegetarian	
TYPE Modern	

CAWS Y GRAIG PEMBROKESHIRE

This goat's cheese is made by Pant Mawr Cheese at Pant Mawr Farm using locally sourced goat's milk. An unpressed hard cheese, matured for up to 12 weeks, it has a textured white rind and an ivory-coloured paste with a dry but slightly crumbly texture. The flavour is mild and nutty with a faint goatiness to it. As the cheese matures, the flavour develops more of a pronounced goat tang.

SIZE	
D. 18cm (7in)	
H. 5cm (2in)	
WEIGHT	
1.25kg (2¾lb)	
SHAPE Round	
MILK Pasteurized goat's	
RENNET Vegetarian	
TYPE Modern	

CHEDDAR
SOMERSET & GLOUCESTERSHIRE

BRITAIN'S BEST-KNOWN CHEESE is named after the village of Cheddar, by Cheddar Gorge in Somerset. It is a cheese with a venerable history: Henry II is known to have ordered a substantial quantity in 1170AD. During the reign of Elizabeth I, Thomas Fuller described the cheeses made at Cheddar as the "best and biggest in England"; so rare and so expensive that they could be found only "at some great man's table". And in the early 18th century, the author Daniel Defoe, in his book *Tour through the Whole of Great Britain*, wrote of visiting the village of Cheddar and described how local dairy farmers pooled their milk to make one large cheese, of which Defoe wrote approvingly, "without all dispute, it is the best cheese that England affords, if not that the whole world affords". Throughout the 17th and 18th centuries, Cheddar cheese commanded premium prices and was seen as a luxury to be enjoyed by the wealthy.

CORPORATION CHEESES

Thanks to their size and the fact that Cheddar requires several months to mature, each cheese demands a considerable investment of resources. For generations, Cheddar was produced in the co-operative tradition observed by Defoe, with dairies pooling their milk supplies, and it consequently became known as a "corporation cheese". The 19th century saw two villages combining their resources to make a memorable Cheddar to celebrate Queen Victoria's wedding: it measured more than 3 metres (9ft) in diameter and weighed a staggering 567kg (1,250lb). Even "ordinary" Cheddars were an impressive size, weighing between 40–52kg (90–120lb).

deep yellow paste

natural rind

dry, flaky texture

MONTGOMERY'S CHEDDAR

SIZE	
D. 32cm (12½in)	
H. 26cm (10½in)	
WEIGHT	
24kg (53lb)	
SHAPE	Round
MILK	Unpasteurized cow's
RENNET	Traditional animal
TYPE	Traditional

MONTGOMERY'S CHEDDAR

The Montgomery family in Somerset makes this artisan Cheddar using its own unpasteurized milk. The curd is passed through a mill, moulded, pressed, dipped in hot water, bandaged in muslin, and matured for at least 11 months. The flaky paste has a rich, long-lasting flavour.

SPECIALIST TECHNIQUES

The defining attribute of Cheddar manufacture is the technique known as "Cheddaring". Slabs of cut curd are layered on top of each other and turned frequently, so that any remaining whey is forced out under the weight and the slabs become pliable. The slabs are then milled – cut into small pieces – before being salted and pressed in moulds.

During the 19th century, the cheesemaker Joseph Harding (1805–76) experimented with Cheddar-making at his farm at Marksbury, paying scrupulous attention to hygiene and charting in great detail the process by which the cheese was made, with particular attention to temperature control. Harding's dictum was: "Cheese is not made in the field, nor in the byre, nor even in the cow, it is made in the dairy." Harding was a key figure in the spreading of Cheddar-making knowledge and techniques, and was consulted by Scottish, Danish, and American cheesemakers.

Harding's invention of the cheese mill helped greatly to standardize Cheddar production. The cheese mill automates the tearing of the curd into small pieces, a process previously done by hand. The mill saves a great deal of time and requires less labour, as well as producing a better-textured cheese.

THE CHEDDAR NAME

Cheddar-making techniques have spread around the world, exported during the 19th and 20th century by emigrants from Britain to countries such as the United States and Canada. The 20th century saw Cheddar-making increasingly standardized and industrialized, both in Britain and abroad. The agricultural depression following World War I put many Cheddar dairies out of business, and, although Cheddar was one of the few cheeses permitted to be made commercially during World War II, farmhouse production dropped sharply with the rise of industrial dairies. In 1939 there were 333 farms in the South-West making Cheddar; by 1948 this had fallen to 57. By 1974 this figure had fallen even further, with only 32 farms in the South-West still producing the cheese. By the 1970s, most Cheddar was being produced from pasteurized milk in the rindless block form beloved of supermarkets.

With no legal protection for the name, "Cheddar" is widely made in countries around the globe, and in many forms only loosely related to the historic cheese. Even in Britain the name Cheddar can legally be applied to both a mass-produced block cheese wrapped in plastic and a lovingly matured, clothbound cheese made by a farmer using unpasteurized milk from his or her own cows. Patrick Rance, the great crusader for the preservation of British cheese, described the situation with

DAYLESFORD CHEDDAR
GLOUCESTERSHIRE

This Cheddar is made in a traditional way by Daylesford Creamery using organic milk from the estate's herd of Friesians, and animal rennet. It is moulded, pressed, bandaged in cloth, and matured for at least nine months, developing a brown natural rind. With a flaky yellow paste, it is sweet and nutty with a long-lasting caramel finish.

SIZE	
D. 25cm (10in)	
H. 40cm (16in)	
WEIGHT	
9kg (20lb)	
SHAPE Truckle	
MILK Unpasteurized organic cow's	
RENNET Vegetarian	
TYPE Traditional	

DITCHEAT HILL CHEDDAR
SOMERSET

Greens of Glastonbury makes this Cheddar using unpasteurized milk from its cows, and a vegetarian rennet. The moulded, pressed cheese is clothbound and matured for at least a year, during which time it develops a natural rind over a pale yellow paste. It has a creamy texture, a mild, slow-burning fullness of flavour, and a sweet finish.

SIZE	
D. 38cm (15in)	
H. 30cm (12in)	
WEIGHT	
25kg (55lb)	
SHAPE Truckle	
MILK Unpasteurized cow's	
RENNET Vegetarian	
TYPE Traditional	

characteristic eloquence: "Even our most generous original gift to humanity, Cheddar, is known to comparatively few people. Most meet it in name alone. What they eat is some hard-pressed rectangular substitute, often foreign, usually emasculated in character and chilled into irredeemable immaturity."

Thankfully, traditional Cheddar-makers today are seeking ways to protect and define the quality of what they produce. A Protected Designation of Origin (PDO) has been given to a group of dairy farmers known as West Country Farmhouse Cheddar. This PDO stipulates that the cheese must be made from local herds reared and milked in Cornwall, Devon, Dorset, or Somerset; that it must contain no colouring, flavouring, or preservatives; that it must be made by traditional methods including "Cheddaring"; and that it must then be matured on the farm where it was made for at least nine months.

BRITAIN'S FAVOURITE

Cheddar continues to be Britain's favourite cheese, popular not only for eating, but also for cooking, with sales of Cheddar dominating the market. In Britain today, many varieties of Cheddar are produced everywhere from small dairies to large commercial creameries. It is a sign of the cheese's enduring popularity that, ever since the British Cheese Awards (see page 185) were founded in 1994, the Cheddar cheese category has consistently seen the largest number of entries.

FARMHOUSE CHEDDARS

In the West Country, where Cheddar's roots lie, a handful of farmhouse cheese-makers continues to make traditional clothbound Cheddar using unpasteurized milk and animal rennet. Each cheese weighs around 22–27kg (50–60lb) and is matured for at least 11 months. Fascinatingly, although these Cheddar cheeses are produced using the same traditional methods, they are all recognizably different from each other in terms of texture and flavour – a tangible reminder of the variety that can be produced by expert cheese-making.

Three Cheddar-makers – Montgomery's (see page 112), Keen's (see opposite), and Westcombe Dairy (see opposite) – have been recognized by the Slow Food movement, an international campaign for the preservation of traditionally produced, high-quality food, which has awarded them a Presidium (a grant for developing and publicizing their product). A world away from the moist, mild curd of supermarket Cheddars, these magnificent farmhouse cheeses, with their complex, rich lingering flavours, are something to treasure.

KEEN'S CHEDDAR SOMERSET

One of the Artisan Somerset Cheesemakers recognized by Slow Food, Keen's makes its traditional Cheddar using unpasteurized milk from its own cows at Moorhayes Farm. A pint starter is used to sour the milk at the beginning of the process, and the clothbound cheese is matured for 12 months. The natural rind covers a dense, moist yellow paste that has a nuttiness of flavour and a tangy bite to it.

SIZE	
D. 32.5cm (13in)	
H. 32.5cm (13in)	
WEIGHT	
26kg (58lb)	
SHAPE Truckle	
MILK Unpasteurized cow's	
RENNET Traditional animal	
TYPE Traditional	

WESTCOMBE CHEDDAR
SOMERSET

A traditional cheddar made by Westcombe Dairy, an Artisan Somerset Cheesemaker recognized by Slow Food, using unpasteurized milk and a pint starter. The moulded, pressed curd is clothbound and matured for 12–18 months, developing a natural rind. The firm yellow paste has a salty-sweet flavour with a tang to it.

SIZE	
D. 25cm (10in)	
H. 25cm (10in)	
WEIGHT	
24kg (53lb)	
SHAPE Truckle	
MILK Pasteurized cow's	
RENNET Traditional animal	
TYPE Traditional	

CHESHIRE SHROPSHIRE

MENTIONED IN THE DOMESDAY BOOK OF 1086AD, Cheshire is considered to be Britain's oldest named cheese. It is a hard-pressed cow's milk cheese associated with the Cheshire plain, which covers parts of Cheshire, Shropshire, and Clwyd. Cattle were grazed on the salty pastures, which were said to impart a particular flavour to the cows' milk and so to the cheese. Cheshire matures excellently, allowing it to travel well, and by the 17th century it was being shipped to London. In 1660 the diarist Samuel Pepys wrote: "Hawley brought a piece of his Cheshire cheese, and we were merry with it", and so well known was the cheese that taverns in the capital were named after it. By the late 18th century, Cheshire cheese had become an important element of the county's economy, and cheese fairs were held in many Cheshire towns.

MASS PRODUCTION

Two world wars and agricultural depression, however, almost destroyed traditional Cheshire production. The industrialization of Cheshire cheese-making and the rise of supermarkets saw factory-produced, plastic-wrapped block Cheshire dominate. Unprotected by law, Cheshire is now made worldwide, and only a handful of English cheesemakers such as Appleby's now produces the traditional clothbound version.

Cheshire's natural colour is pale cream, but "red" Cheshire, actually orange in colour, is also made by colouring the paste with carrot juice or annatto. Traditional Cheshire had a period of "finishing off", which involved skewering the cheeses midway through maturation, renewing the cheesecloth, and leaving them to age. This process inevitably led to the rise of a blue version, and Blue Cheshire cheese is still made today.

APPLEBY'S CHESHIRE

SIZE	
D. 30cm (12in)	
H. 26cm (10½in)	
WEIGHT	
22kg (48½lb)	
SHAPE Round	
MILK Unpasteurized cow's	
RENNET Vegetarian	
TYPE Traditional	

"red" paste

natural rind

flaky texture

APPLEBY'S CHESHIRE

Appleby's Dairy of Hawkstone Abbey Farm in Shropshire
makes this cheese using milk from its own cows. The
moulded, pressed cheeses are wrapped in calico and
matured for two to six months. It has a flaky, moist
texture and gentle yet complex and lingering flavour.

CHEVINGTON NORTHUMBERLAND

The Northumberland Cheese Company at Blagdon makes this cheese using locally sourced Jersey cow's milk from Wheelbirks' Jersey herd at Stocksfield, the oldest Jersey herd in Northumberland. The cheese is matured for between 10–12 weeks, during which time it develops a knobbly brown natural rind, dotted with white mould, over a smooth yellow paste. The paste is moist, and the cheese has a mild, creamy flavour.

SIZE	
D. 20cm (8in)	
H. 5cm (2in)	
WEIGHT	
2–2.5kg (4½–5½lb)	
SHAPE Wheel	
MILK Pasteurized cow's	
RENNET Vegetarian	
TYPE Modern	

CHEVIOT NORTHUMBERLAND

Named after the Cheviot Hills, this cheese is made by the Northumberland Cheese Company, established by Mark Robertson in 1984, and now based at Blagdon. The dairy uses locally sourced milk, which can be traced back to individual farms. A pressed cheese, it is wrapped and matured for nine months. The resulting cheese has a pale yellow paste, with a smooth, moist texture and a buttery flavour.

SIZE	
D. 20cm (8in)	
H. 5cm (2in)	
WEIGHT	
2–2½kg (4½–5½lb)	
SHAPE Wheel	
MILK Pasteurized cow's	
RENNET Vegetarian	
TYPE Modern	

CLOCHANDIGHTER
ABERDEENSHIRE

This hard cow's cheese is made by Devenick Dairy using pasteurized milk from its cows. The milk is curdled, drained, cut, milled, moulded, and pressed, then set aside to mature for three months. As it matures, it develops a pale natural rind over the pale yellow paste. The texture is moist and crumbly, and it has a mild, fresh flavour.

SIZE	
D. 24cm (9½in)	
H. 12cm (4¾in)	
WEIGHT	
6kg (13lb)	
SHAPE Round	
MILK Pasteurized cow's	
RENNET Vegetarian	
TYPE Modern	

COOLEA CO CORK

Coolea Farmhouse Cheese at Macroom has been making this cheese since the late 1970s. The recipe is in the Gouda style and involves washing the curd, heating it, moulding, pressing, and salting in brine. The cheese is matured for around six months, during which time it develops a smooth deep yellow rind over a firm yellow paste. The taste, initially salty and savoury, has a rich caramel sweetness that lingers.

SIZE	
D. 25cm (10in) & 35cm (13¾in)	
H. 10cm (4in)	
WEIGHT	
4.5kg (10lb) & 8.5–9kg (18–20lb)	
SHAPE Millstone	
MILK Pasteurized cow's	
RENNET Traditional animal	
TYPE Modern	

COQUETDALE NORTHUMBERLAND

Mark Robertson of the Northumberland Cheese Company created this hand-made cheese on the Blagdon Estate in South Northumberland. The milk comes from the estate's own herd of Red Poll and Friesian cows, with each batch fully traceable. A mould-ripened cheese with a natural rind, Coquetdale has a supple texture to its paste and a rich, complex flavour with a noticeably long fruity finish.

SIZE	
D. 30cm (12in)	
H. 10cm (4in)	
WEIGHT	
2–2.5kg (4½–5½lb)	
SHAPE	Wheel
MILK	Pasteurized cow's
RENNET	Vegetarian
TYPE	Traditional

CORNISH CRUMBLY CORNWALL

Whalesborough Farm Foods, near Bude, makes this cow's milk cheese, inspired, as the name suggests, by the crumbly Lancashire style of cheese. The moulded curd is pressed under its own weight and matured for four weeks. During this time, the cheese develops a knobbly brown rind, blotched with different–coloured moulds, over a pale yellow paste. It is fine-grained and crumbly, with a mild and milky flavour.

SIZE	
D. 20cm (8in)	
H. 6cm (2½in)	
WEIGHT	
1.5kg (3lb 3oz)	
SHAPE	Round
MILK	Pasteurized cow's
RENNET	Vegetarian
TYPE	Modern

STORING HARD CHEESES

Hard cheeses can be matured for many months if they are stored in the right conditions. As they age, they develop in flavour and the texture becomes drier.

CORNISH YARG CORNWALL

With a strikingly patterned rind (due to being wrapped in nettle leaves), this Cornish cheese is hand-made following a 17th-century recipe that was rediscovered and made by a couple called Gray. The cheese's West Country-sounding name is "Gray" spelt backwards. Today, it is produced by Lynher Dairies in Cornwall using the dairy's own milk. It has a smooth paste and a mild, slightly mushroomy flavour.

SIZE	
D. 28cm (11in)	
H. 9cm (3½in)	
WEIGHT	
3kg (6½lb)	
SHAPE Wheel	
MILK Pasteurized cow's	
RENNET Vegetarian	
TYPE Modern	

COTHERSTONE DURHAM

A traditional Dales cheese, Cotherstone is hand-made by Joan Cross at Quarry House Farm near Barnard Castle. There has long been a tradition in the Dales of keeping cows and making cheese from their milk, and Joan grew up watching her mother make cheese. Matured for one to three months, Cotherstone has a natural rind, with some white and blue moulds on it, a creamy texture, and a rich, buttery flavour.

SIZE	
D. 7.5–22cm (3– 8½in)	
H. 7.5cm (3in)	
WEIGHT	
500g–3kg (1lb 2oz–6½lb)	
SHAPE Wheel	
MILK Pasteurized cow's	
RENNET Vegetarian	
TYPE Modern	

CROGLIN CUMBRIA

Thornby Moor Dairy at Crofton Hall, Thursby, makes this hard sheep's cheese seasonally, using locally sourced sheep's milk between February and October. The cheese is matured for at least a month, and is sold at an older age as the season progresses. It develops a natural rind over a pale paste, with a delicate sweetness and nutty flavour when young, becoming drier and fuller in flavour as it ages.

SIZE	
D. 5cm (2in) & 9cm (3½in)	
H. 20cm (8in)	
WEIGHT	
250g (9oz) & 1.2kg (2¾lb)	
SHAPE Curling stone	
MILK Unpasteurized sheep's	
RENNET Vegetarian	
TYPE Modern	

CHEESE CHAMPION

Patrick Rance's Wells Stores at Streatley was a treasure house of superb cheeses. Generous with his considerable knowledge, Patrick Rance (1917-1999) was a kind man, widely respected and held in deep affection. Many farmhouse cheesemakers still remember the help he gave them. On hearing of Charles Martell's plan to revive Double Gloucester, for example, Patrick sent him a blank cheque, and there are many similar anecdotes telling of his help and generosity.

Patrick once said that "a slice of good cheese is never just a thing to eat. It is a slice of history." He wrote knowledgeably and from the heart about farmhouse cheeses and became an eloquent and influential spokesman for the movement to preserve Britain's traditional cheese-making heritage.

PATRICK RANCE
Rance battled to save British farmhouse cheeses from extinction.

CROMAL INVERNESS

This organic cheese is made by Connage Highland Dairy at Milton of Connage farm The dairy uses milk from its own organic dairy herd, made up mostly of Holstein–Friesian with Jersey crosses and Norwegian Reds. The curd is "Cheddared", and pressed and sold at four weeks, when it has a pale rind over a creamy yellow paste with a moist, crumbly texture and a very mild flavour.

SIZE	
D. 25cm (10in) & 40cm (16in)	
H. 9cm (3½in) & 14cm (5½in)	
WEIGHT	
4.5kg (10lb) & 14kg (31lb)	
SHAPE Round	
MILK Pasteurized organic cow's	
RENNET Vegetarian	
TYPE Modern	

CUDDY'S CAVE NORTHUMBERLAND

Doddington Dairy on North Doddington Farm, Wooler, makes this hard cheese using unpasteurized cow's milk from its own herd of cows, and traditional animal rennet. Made in the Dales style, the cheese is matured for between two to five months, during which time it develops a brown natural rind. The pale yellow paste has a smooth texture, and the cheese has a mild, nutty flavour with a long finish.

SIZE	
D. 23cm (9in)	
H. 6cm (2½in)	
WEIGHT	
4kg (9lb)	
SHAPE Round	
MILK Unpasteurized cow's	
RENNET Traditional animal	
TYPE Modern	

CUMBERLAND FARMHOUSE
CUMBRIA

Thornby Moor Dairy, Thursby, makes this cheese using locally sourced unpasteurized cow's milk. The moulded, pressed curd is clothbound and matured for at least two months, although it is at its best at five months. Under the natural rind, the pale yellow paste has a smooth texture and a rounded flavour, developing as the cheese matures.

SIZE	
D. 10–23cm (4–9in)	
H. 10–20cm (4–8in)	
WEIGHT	
1–9kg (2¼–20lb)	
SHAPE Truckle	
MILK Unpasteurized cow's	
RENNET Vegetarian	
TYPE Modern	

CURWORTHY DEVON

Based on an old 17th-century recipe, Curworthy is hand-made by Rachel Stevens on her farm in Devon using milk from her herd of Holstein–Friesians. Depending on the size of the cheese, Curworthy is matured for between two to four months. It develops a natural rind, but is also available coated in black wax (as shown here). It is a low-acid cheese with a supple texture and a long-lasting buttery flavour.

SIZE	
D. 9cm–20cm (3½–8in)	
H. 6cm–10cm (2½in–4in)	
WEIGHT	
450g–2.2kg (1–5lb)	
SHAPE Cylinder	
MILK Pasteurized cow's	
RENNET Traditional animal	
TYPE Traditional	

DEESIDER ABERDEENSHIRE

Devenick Dairy in Banchory-Devenick, near Aberdeen, makes this cheese using pasteurized milk from the dairy farm's own herd of cows. The milk is curdled, drained, moulded, and pressed, then the cheese is coated in green wax to protect it and retain moisture. Set aside to mature for six months, it develops a moist but firm pale yellow paste inside the wax coating and has a mild flavour.

SIZE	
D. 12cm (4¾in)	
H. 3.5cm (1¼in)	
WEIGHT	
1.3kg (3lb)	
SHAPE Wheel	
MILK Pasteurized cow's	
RENNET Vegetarian	
TYPE Modern	

DELAMERE DISTINCTIVE
CHESHIRE

Delamere Dairy makes this mature goat's cheese using goat's milk sourced from various UK suppliers. A hard-pressed cheese, it is made in a large round, pressed for 18 hours, and matured for 9–12 months. The paste is ivory with a moist, crumbly texture, while the flavour is light but distinctly goaty with a nuttiness to the taste.

SIZE	
D. 35cm (13¾in)	
H. 14cm (5½in)	
WEIGHT	
14kg (31lb)	
SHAPE Round	
MILK Pasteurized goat's	
RENNET Vegetarian	
TYPE Modern	

DERBY SAGE WEST MIDLANDS

Fowlers of Earlswood has been making Derby cheese since 1840. It makes this cheese from pasteurized cow's milk using a recipe that is more than 100 years old. As the milled curd is placed in the moulds, a layer of chopped sage is added, giving the cheese a characteristic band of dark green flecks. The cheese has a firm, moist yellow paste, with the sage adding a herbal note to the creamy taste of the cheese.

SIZE	
D. 20cm (8in)	
H. 10cm (4in)	
WEIGHT	
1.5kg (3lb 3oz)	
SHAPE Half-moon	
MILK Pasteurized cow's	
RENNET Vegetarian	
TYPE Traditional	

DESMOND CO CORK

This Swiss-style cheese is made by the West Cork Natural Cheese Company. It is made only during the summer months, using milk from the Newmarket Co-operative. It is a thermophilic cheese (as are Gruyère and Emmenthal) made with a yoghurt-like starter and matured for at least a year. Under the natural rind, the rich golden paste is firm and dry with a powerful, long-lingering flavour.

SIZE	
D. 32cm (12½in)	
H. 10–13cm (4–5in)	
WEIGHT	
7kg (15½lb)	
SHAPE Round	
MILK Unpasteurized cow's	
RENNET Traditional animal & vegetarian	
TYPE Modern	

DEVON OKE DEVON

Curworthy Cheese at Stockbeare Farm makes this cheese using unpasteurized cow's milk from the farm's own herd of Friesians, and uses animal rennet to curdle the milk. The curd is scalded, cut, moulded, bathed in brine, and matured for at least three months. During maturation, the cheese develops a golden natural rind, dusted with white mould, over a smooth pale yellow paste which has a full, well-rounded flavour.

SIZE	
D. 14–20cm (5½–8in)	
H. 6–13cm (2½–5in)	
WEIGHT	
1–4.5kg (2¼–10lb)	
SHAPE Round	
MILK Pasteurized cow's	
RENNET Traditional animal	
TYPE Modern	

DEVON SAGE DEVON

This flavoured cheese is made for Country Cheeses by Rachel Stephens using milk from her Friesians. Chopped sage is added at the beginning of the cheese-making process, with the curd then moulded, pressed, and brined. Matured for three to four months, the paste is moist and yellow inside a green wax coating. It is flecked with green from the sage, with the cheese both smelling and tasting of the herb.

SIZE	
D. 19.5cm (7½in)	
H. 7.5cm (3in)	
WEIGHT	
2.25kg (5lb)	
SHAPE Round	
MILK Pasteurized cow's	
RENNET Vegetarian	
TYPE Modern	

DODDINGTON NORTHUMBERLAND

This Northumbrian hard cheese is made by Doddington Dairy, North Doddington
Farm, Wooler. The dairy uses unpasteurized milk from the farm's cows and traditional
animal rennet, and matures the cheese for 12–14 months. Doddington has a dark
reddish-brown natural rind and a dry deep yellow paste with a faintly crystalline
texture. The flavour is rich and salty-sweet with a long finish.

SIZE	
D. 23cm (9in) & 32cm (12½in)	
H. 11cm (4½in)	
WEIGHT	
5kg (11lb) & 10kg (22lb)	
SHAPE Round	
MILK Unpasteurized cow's	
RENNET Traditional animal	
TYPE Modern	

DOUBLE BERKELEY
GLOUCESTERSHIRE

Charles Martell revived the making of this cheese (documented in 1796 as being made
in the Berkeley district of Gloucestershire). Annatto is added to create the distinctive
mottled orange-and-white paste. The curd is moulded, pressed, and matured for two
to three months. It has a natural rind, a creamy texture, and a mild, sweet flavour.

SIZE	
D. 22cm (8½in)	
H. 7cm (2¾in)	
WEIGHT	
2.25kg (5lb)	
SHAPE Round	
MILK Pasteurized cow's	
RENNET Vegetarian	
TYPE Traditional	

DOUBLE GLOUCESTER
GLOUCESTERSHIRE & SHROPSHIRE

THE FERTILE COUNTY OF GLOUCESTERSHIRE is associated with Single and Double Gloucester cheeses. Historically, these were made using milk from Gloucester cattle, a handsome horned brown-black animal with a distinctive white stripe down its back and along its belly. The Gloucester was, and still is, valued for its gentle temperament and for producing good beef and milk – the latter, with its small fat globules, is ideal for cheese-making.

SINGLE AND DOUBLE GLOUCESTER

The distinction between the two cheeses arose at the end of the 18th century: Double Gloucester was exported outside the county, with cheese merchants touring local farms to check the quality of their produce, while Single was reserved for consumption at home. Double Gloucester is a bigger, thicker cheese than Single, which may be where the names originated.

The naming may also derive from the milk that goes to make up the cheeses. Single Gloucester has a lower fat content than Double Gloucester, being made with partially skimmed milk. Double Gloucester is richer, made from either the whole milk of two milkings or with milk and additional cream. Double Gloucester is an older, harder cheese, with annatto (an orange plant extract) added to produce the characteristic pale tangerine colour. In 1783 William Marshall, in his *Rural Economy of Gloucestershire*, described in detail the making of Gloucester cheese. He described cheeses being piled two or four high as they matured, with the rind already tough enough at one month for them to be "thrown about like old cheeses". As a notoriously

APPLEBY'S DOUBLE GLOUCESTER

SIZE	
D. 32cm (12½in)	
H. 15cm (6in)	
WEIGHT	
13kg (28½ lb)	
SHAPE Round	
MILK Unpasteurized cow's	
RENNET Vegetarian	
TYPE Traditional	

orange paste

smooth, firm texture

natural rind

APPLEBY'S DOUBLE GLOUCESTER

Appleby's of Shropshire makes this cheese using
unpasteurized cow's milk. To create the close texture,
the curd is only lightly broken. The cheese is matured
for 10–14 weeks, while annatto gives it colour, resulting
in a firm-textured cheese with a full, sweet flavour.

tough-rinded, hard-pressed cheese, sold at four to six months, Double Gloucester travelled well, and was exported around the country by barge, horse, or wagon. Its toughness lent itself to cheese-rolling, a centuries-old Gloucestershire custom which is still practised every year at Coopers Hill, near Brockworth.

GLOUCESTER REVIVAL

During the 20th century, production of Double Gloucester became factory- rather than farm-centred. As demand for high milk yields grew, herds of Gloucester cattle dwindled steadily until the 1970s, when a cheesemaker called Charles Martell revived the Gloucester Cattle Society and set about making traditional Double Gloucester. Today, a handful of Gloucestershire cheese-makers produces farmhouse Double and Single Gloucester cheeses. In 1997 Single Gloucester was given Protected Definition of Origin (PDO) by the European Union, and can now be made only in Gloucestershire on farms with a pedigree herd of Old Gloucester. The Slow Food movement, which campaigns to protect traditional food producers, awarded a Presidium grant to Double and Single Gloucester in 2004. Gloucester cattle are still classed as "endangered", but numbers are slowly recovering, with more than 730 cows now registered.

DOUBLE GLOUCESTER
GLOUCESTERSHIRE

Charles Martell (see above) makes this Double Gloucester using milk from his Old Gloucester cows. Annatto is added to create the characteristic apricot-coloured paste, and the cheese develops a thick natural rind as it matures for four to six months. The paste inside is soft with a moist, creamy texture and a sweet, milky mildness of flavour.

SIZE	
D. 22cm (8½in)	
H. 7cm (2¾in)	
WEIGHT	
2.25kg (5lb)	
SHAPE Round	
MILK Pasteurized & unpasteurized cow's	
RENNET Vegetarian	
TYPE Traditional	

DOUBLE WORCESTER
WORCESTERSHIRE

The county of Worcestershire's equivalent to a Double Gloucester, this is made by Ansteys at Broomhall Farm. Annatto is added to give it the distinctive orange colour. The curd is double-cut and double-milled to give a finer texture. Matured for six months, it has a natural rind over a smooth, firm paste and a subtle fullness of flavour.

SIZE	
D. 20cm (8in)	
H. 15cm (6in)	
WEIGHT	
3.5kg (7½lb)	
SHAPE Round	
MILK Pasteurized cow's	
RENNET Vegetarian	
TYPE Modern	

DRUMLIN CO CAVAN

Corleggy Cheese makes this Irish cheese using unpasteurized cow's milk from a local farmer. The name comes from the drumlin pastures surrounding Corleggy on which the cows graze. Matured for at least six weeks, Drumlin develops a knobbly golden-brown rind over a firm, moist yellow paste with a rich, savoury flavour. It is also available smoked and flavoured with garlic and red pepper, cumin seeds, and peppercorns.

SIZE	
D. 8cm (3¼in) & 16cm (6½in)	
H. 7cm (2¾in) & 45cm (17½in)	
WEIGHT	
350g (12oz) & 900g (2lb)	
SHAPE Cylinder & round	
MILK Unpasteurized cow's	
RENNET Vegetarian	
TYPE Modern	

DRUMLOCH WHEEL ARGYLL

Inverloch Cheese makes this hard cow's cheese at its creamery at Campbeltown, the Mull of Kintyre. It is made with Guernsey cow's milk from a herd grazed on the shores of West Loch Tarbet which, in the summer months especially, produces a rich yellow milk. The moulded, pressed cheese is coated in green wax and matured for a year. Under the wax, the firm yellow paste has a creamy texture and a buttery savouriness.

SIZE	
D. 15m (6in)	
H. 15cm (6in)	
WEIGHT	
3kg (6½lb)	
SHAPE Cylinder	
MILK Pasteurized cow's	
RENNET Vegetarian	
TYPE Modern	

DUDDLESWELL WEST SUSSEX

High Weald Dairy at Tremains Farm in Horsted Keynes makes this cheese using sheep's milk sourced from dedicated farms. Inspired by the tradition of the Dales cheeses, made by farmhouses as a way of storing milk, the cheese is matured for three months, developing a natural golden rind over a pale cream-coloured paste. The texture is smooth and creamy, while the flavour has a mild, nutty sweetness.

SIZE	
D. 24cm (9½in)	
H. 7–8cm (2¾–3¼in)	
WEIGHT	
3.2kg (7lb)	
SHAPE Wheel	
MILK Pasteurized sheep's	
RENNET Vegetarian	
TYPE Modern	

DUNLOP AYRSHIRE

Dunlop, Scotland's indigenous hard cheese, was first made in the late 17th century. This variety is made by Ann Dorward at Dunlop Dairy at West Clerkland Farm, Stewarton, who first revived this traditional cheese using the rich milk from the farm's own Ayrshire cows. Matured for six months, it develops a pale primrose yellow paste with a firm, moist texure. The flavour is full with a lingering salty-sweetness to it.

SIZE	
D. 4–30cm (1½–12in)	
H. 6–30cm (2½–12in)	
WEIGHT	
400g–20kg (14oz–44lb)	
SHAPE Round	
MILK Pasteurized cow's	
RENNET Vegetarian	
TYPE Traditional	

DUTCHMAN WEST SUSSEX

This impressive-sized cheese is made on Old Plaw Hatch Farm, a biodynamic farm, using unpasteurized milk from the farm's cows, only when they are producing enough milk. As the name suggests, this Gouda-style cheese is the legacy of a Dutch cheesemaker. Matured for three months, it develops a golden natural rind and a pale mild-tasting paste, and is available plain or flavoured with cumin or peppercorns.

SIZE	
D. 35cm (13¾in) & 43cm (17in)	
H. 8cm (3¼in) & 10cm (4in)	
WEIGHT	
9kg (20lb) & 18kg (40lb)	
SHAPE Wheel	
MILK Unpasteurized cow's	
RENNET Vegetarian	
TYPE Modern	

ELGAR MATURE WORCESTERSHIRE

This hard clothbound cheese is made by Lightwood Cheese using unpasteurized cow's milk. The curd is moulded in cloth-lined moulds, pressed, dipped in hot water, then pressed again, dried, and matured for 9–12 months. It has a golden-brown rind, flecked with white and orange moulds, and a deep yellow paste. The texture is firm but creamy, and the flavour mellow with a touch of old-fashioned sharpness.

SIZE	
D. 20cm (8in)	
H. 13cm (5in)	
WEIGHT	
3.8kg (8½lb)	
SHAPE Circular truckle	
MILK Unpasteurized cow's	
RENNET Vegetarian	
TYPE Modern	

FOSSEWAY FLEECE SOMERSET

Made by the Somerset Cheese Company at Ditcheat Hill Farm, this hard sheep's cheese is named after the local Fosseway. The curds are moulded, pressed overnight, and matured for between 4–12 months, during which time the cheese develops a natural brown rind, splotched with white mould. The pale creamy-white paste has a smooth, firm, waxy texture and a mild but lasting nutty flavour.

SIZE	
D. 18cm (7in) & 25cm (10in)	
H. 7.5cm (3in)	
WEIGHT	
2kg (4½lb) & 3.5kg (7½lb)	
SHAPE Wheel	
MILK Pasteurized sheep's	
RENNET Vegetarian	
TYPE Modern	

GABRIEL CO CORK

One of a handful of Swiss-style "thermophilic" cheeses made in Ireland and Britain, this variety is made by the West Cork Natural Cheese Company, only during the summer. It uses a yoghurt-like starter and milk from the Newmarket Co-operative where the cheese is made. Matured for at least a year, it develops a natural rind and a hard, dry paste with a granular texture and a slow-burning, powerful fruity flavour.

SIZE	
D. 32cm (12½in)	
H. 10–12cm (4–4¾in)	
WEIGHT	
7kg (15½lb)	
SHAPE Round	
MILK Unpasteurized cow's	
RENNET Traditional animal & vegetarian	
TYPE Modern	

GALLYBAGGER ISLE OF WIGHT

Created and made by Isle of Wight Cheese, this cheese draws its name from a local dialect word for "scarecrow". Cheesemaker Richard Hodgson uses an Italian starter culture added to unpasteurized Guernsey cow's milk. The pressed cheese is matured for seven months, during which time it develops a dark brown natural rind over a rich yellow paste. The cheese has a long-lasting full, sweet, nutty flavour.

SIZE	
D. 25cm (10in)	
H. 13cm (5in)	
WEIGHT	
5kg (11lb)	
SHAPE Round	
MILK Unpasteurized cow's	
RENNET Vegetarian	
TYPE Modern	

GLEBE BRETHAN CO LOUTH

This impressive Gruyère-type cheese is made at the Tiernan Family Farm using unpasteurized milk from the farm's Montbeliarde herd, and animal rennet. The large cheeses are matured on spruce wood for 6–18 months. During maturation, the cheese forms a natural brown rind over a dense, smooth yellow paste. Depending on age, the flavour ranges from fruity and buttery to a fuller, spicier taste when mature.

SIZE	
D. 66cm (26in)	
H. 10cm (4in)	
WEIGHT	
45kg (99lb)	
SHAPE Wheel	
MILK Unpasteurized cow's	
RENNET Traditional animal	
TYPE Modern	

GODMINSTER SOMERSET

This organic Cheddar is made for Godminster Farm using pasteurized organic cow's milk. The curd is "Cheddared", and the cheese is made in 20kg (44lb) blocks, which are matured for 12 months, then remilled and formed into assorted shapes and sizes, and coated in Soil Association-certified burgundy-coloured wax. Under the wax coating, the pale yellow paste has a fine-grained, moist texture and a salty-sweet flavour.

SIZE	
D. 7.5–15.5cm (3–6¼in)	
H. 4.5–10cm (1¾–4in)	
WEIGHT	
400g–2kg (14oz–4½lb)	
SHAPE Round & heart	
MILK Pasteurized organic cow's	
RENNET Vegetarian	
TYPE Traditional	

GRANITE CITY ABERDEENSHIRE

Devenick Dairy in Banchory-Devenick, near Aberdeen, makes this distinctive-looking cheese using pasteurized milk from the dairy farm's own herd of cows. The milk is curdled, drained, moulded, and pressed, then the cheese is coated in green and red wax, and set aside to mature for six months. The pale yellow paste inside the wax coating is moist and firm, and has a mild, creamy flavour.

SIZE	
D. 12cm (4¾in)	
H. 5cm (2in)	
WEIGHT	
550g (1¼lb)	
SHAPE	Wheel
MILK	Pasteurized cow's
RENNET	Vegetarian
TYPE	Modern

GUNSTONE GOAT DEVON

Norsworthy Dairy in Crediton makes this goat's cheese using unpasteurized milk from its own herd of Saanen, Toggenburg, and British Alpine goats. Annatto is added to the milk to give the cheese its pale apricot-coloured paste. The curd is washed, and the cheese is matured for two months, developing a natural golden rind. It has a moist paste and a mild, full, sweet flavour with a touch of goat.

SIZE	
D. 18cm (7in)	
H. 11cm (4½in)	
WEIGHT	
2–2.5kg (4½–5½lb)	
SHAPE	Round
MILK	Unpasteurized goat's
RENNET	Vegetarian
TYPE	Modern

HAMPSHIRE ROSE WILTSHIRE

This hard cheese is made by Loosehanger Farmhouse Cheeses at Home Farm, Salisbury. It is produced using Ayrshire milk from a single herd, which Loosehanger pasteurizes during the winter months, but not during the summer when the milk is at its rich best. Matured for at least six months, it has a golden rind and a firm ivory-coloured paste. The flavour is full and salty-sweet with a lingering sweet finish.

SIZE	
D. 19.5cm (7½in)	
H. 10–11cm (4–4½in)	
WEIGHT	
3.5–4kg (7½–9lb)	
SHAPE Wheel	
MILK Seasonally unpasteurized	
RENNET Vegetarian	
TYPE Modern	

HAREFIELD GLOUCESTERSHIRE

Diana Smart at Old Ley Farm, noted for her Gloucester cheeses, also makes this hard cow's cheese using a mixture of skimmed and whole milk. The scalded curd is milled, dry-salted by hand, moulded, and pressed. It is then matured for two years, during which time the cheese develops a craggy-textured brown rind over a dull yellow paste. The texture is hard and dry, and the flavour powerful with a distinct tang.

SIZE	
D. 25cm (10in)	
H. 5cm (2in)	
WEIGHT	
2.2kg (5lb)	
SHAPE Wheel	
MILK Unpasteurized cow's	
RENNET Vegetarian	
TYPE Modern	

HAWKSTON SUFFOLK

Rodwell Farm Dairy, Baylham, makes this cheese using unpasteurized milk from Holstein–Friesians. The milk is ripened and curdled, then chopped, scalded, cut, and turned. It is placed in cloth-lined moulds and pressed, muslin-bandaged, and matured for two to three weeks. The matured cheese has a natural brown rind, blotched with white mould, and a firm, pale yellow paste with a mild, lemony flavour.

SIZE	
D. 25cm (10in)	
H. 10cm (4in)	
WEIGHT	
4.3–5kg (9½–11lb)	
SHAPE Wheel	
MILK Unpasteurized cow's	
RENNET Vegetarian	
TYPE Modern	

HEREFORD HOP GLOUCESTERSHIRE

Created and made by Charle Martell at Dymock, close to the Herefordshire border, this cheese has a distinctive appearance due to the layer of toasted hops that encrust it. Made with full-fat pasteurized milk, it is moulded, coated with hops, and matured for three months. The resulting cheese has a firm pale paste with a mild flavour, contrasting with the texture and ale note from the hops.

SIZE	
D. 22cm (8½in)	
H. 7cm (2¾in)	
WEIGHT	
2.25kg (5lb)	
SHAPE Wheel	
MILK Pasteurized cow's	
RENNET Vegetarian	
TYPE Modern	

INVERLOCH ARGYLL

This goat's cheese is made by Inverloch Cheese at its creamery at Campbeltown, the Mull of Kintyre. Locally sourced goat's milk is used to make the cheese, which is made only during the months when the goats are in milk. The moulded cheese is pressed and matured for four to six months, then coated in red wax. The white paste is firm and smooth, and it has a nutty sweetness without being overwhelmingly goaty.

SIZE	
D. 15cm (6in)	
H. 15cm (6in)	
WEIGHT	
3kg (6½lb)	
SHAPE Wheel	
MILK Pasteurized goat's	
RENNET Vegetarian	
TYPE Modern	

ISLE OF MULL ISLE OF MULL

This hard cheese is made by Isle of Mull Cheeses at Sgriob-Ruadh Farm Dairy, Tobermory, using unpasteurized milk from the farm's closed herd of cows, and traditional animal rennet. The curd is milled, salted, moulded, and pressed, then cloth-wrapped and matured in the cellar for six months. It has a textured brown natural rind over a yellow paste, and a powerful, complex, lingering flavour.

SIZE	
D. 5–28cm (2–11in)	
H. 9–23cm (3½–9in)	
WEIGHT	
400g–25kg (14oz–55lb)	
SHAPE Truckle & cylinder	
MILK Unpasteurized cow's	
RENNET Traditional animal	
TYPE Modern	

THICK SKINS

Hard cheeses such as this Berkswell (see page 102) often develop thick, tough rinds, which take their shape and texture from the containers in which they are moulded.

JUNAS SOMERSET

Alham Wood in West Cranmore makes this organic cheese on its farm, using unpasteurized milk from its own herd of water buffalo. Junas is, in fact, named after the matriarch of the herd. The cheese is matured for four to eight months and has a pale brown rind, which is textured and blotched. The ivory paste inside has a dense, moist texture and a lactic flavour with a salty-sweetness to it.

SIZE	
D. 18cm (7in)	
H. 10cm (4in)	
WEIGHT	
900g–1.1kg (2–2½lb)	
SHAPE Round	
MILK Unpasteurized organic buffalo's	
RENNET Vegetarian	
TYPE Modern	

KELSAE ROXBURGHSHIRE

This Scottish hard cheese is made by Stichill Jerseys, at Garden Cottage Farm, using unpasteurized milk from the farm's Jersey cows. The milk is coagulated, then the curd is cut, milled, dry-salted, placed in cheesecloth-lined moulds, and pressed for seven days, before being wrapped and matured for four to six months. The matured cheese has a pale yellow paste with a moist, crumbly texture and mild, creamy flavour.

SIZE	
D. 20cm (8in)	
H. 20cm (8in)	
WEIGHT	
4kg (9lb)	
SHAPE Wheel	
MILK Unpasteurized cow's	
RENNET Vegetarian	
TYPE Modern	

KIELDER NORTHUMBERLAND

Made by the Northumberland Cheese Company at Blagdon, this cheese is named after Kielder Forest. It is made from locally sourced Jersey cow's milk from Wheelbirks' Jersey herd at Stocksfield, the oldest Jersey herd in Northumberland. A young unpressed cheese, Kielder is matured for six weeks. At this age, the cheese has a pale yellow paste with a smooth, moist texture and a mild flavour.

SIZE	
D. 20cm (8in)	
H. 5cm (2in)	
WEIGHT	
2–2.5kg (4½–5½lb)	
SHAPE Wheel	
MILK Pasteurized cow's	
RENNET Vegetarian	
TYPE Modern	

KILLEEN COW CO GALWAY

Killeen Farmhouse Cheeses at Killeen Millhouse, Balllinasloe, makes this Irish cheese using milk from a neighbour's herd of cows. The cheese is made following a Gouda-style recipe, with the curd being washed, then moulded and pressed. It is ready to eat at 10 weeks. A 10-week-old cheese has a creamy texture and mild flavour, whereas at 10 months the texture is drier and the flavour fuller, although still sweet.

SIZE	
D. 30cm (12in)	
H. 10cm (4in)	
WEIGHT	
5kg (11lb)	
SHAPE Round	
MILK Pasteurized cow's	
RENNET Traditional animal	
TYPE Modern	

KILLEEN GOAT CO GALWAY

This Irish goat's cheese is made by Killeen Farmhouse Cheeses, Ballinasloe, using milk from its goats. The cheese is made following a Gouda-style recipe, with the curd washed, then moulded, pressed, and matured for at least eight weeks, developing a golden-brown natural rind. At this age, the white paste has a creamy texture and a sweetness; at 10 months, the texture is drier, with a more complex flavour.

SIZE	
D. 30cm (12in)	
H. 10cm (4in)	
WEIGHT	
5kg (11lb)	
SHAPE Round	
MILK Pasteurized cow's	
RENNET Vegetarian	
TYPE Modern	

KNOCKANORE CO WATERFORD

This is made by Knockanore Irish Farmhouse Cheese using unpasteurized milk from its Friesian cows. Once formed, the hard-pressed cheese is matured for at least six months. The smoked version, pictured here, is smoked over oak in a traditional kiln, giving the rind a brown colour. Aside from smoked, the cheese is available in other flavoured versions: black pepper and chives, garlic and chives, and garlic and herbs.

SIZE	
D. 20cm (8in)	
H. 10cm (4in)	
WEIGHT	
3kg (6½ lb)	
SHAPE Wheel	
MILK Unpasteurized cow's	
RENNET Vegetarian	
TYPE Modern	

LAMMAS CEREDIGION

Caws Celtica make this Welsh cheese using unpasteurized milk from its flock of sheep. The cheese is matured for at least a month, at which point it has a creamy, moist texture; as it matures, it becomes drier and the flavour more pronounced. It has a golden-brown natural rind and a pale paste with a noticeable taste of sheep. It is also available flavoured with spices, including celery seeds, cumin, and black pepper.

SIZE	
D. 8–25cm (3¼–10in)	
H. 6–9cm (2½–3½in)	
WEIGHT	
250g–4.5kg (9oz–10lb)	
SHAPE Round & wheel	
MILK Unpasteurized cow's	
RENNET Vegetarian	
TYPE Modern	

LANARK WHITE LANARKSHIRE

This cheese is made at Walston Braehead in Scotland by Humphrey Errington, using unpasteurized milk from his own ewes. Noted for his blue cheeses, Humphrey here drew on the tradition of unpressed farmhouse cheeses. The sheep's milk curd is drained, moulded, unpressed, and matured for three months. As its name suggests, it is indeed a white cheese, with a moist creamy paste and a fresh, citrus tang.

SIZE	
D. 22cm (8½in)	
H. 10cm (4in)	
WEIGHT	
3kg (6½lb)	
SHAPE Wheel	
MILK Unpasteurized sheep's	
RENNET Vegetarian	
TYPE Modern	

LANCASHIRE LANCASHIRE

ONE OF BRITAIN'S "TERRITORIAL" CHEESES, Lancashire developed its own identity in the 18th century, distinguishing itself from neighbouring Cheshire. Traditional Lancashire has the softest texture of all England's hard-pressed cow's milk cheeses. Uniquely among English cheeses, it was produced by mixing batches of curds from two or three days' milking. One reason for this is thought to be the small size of Lancashire herds, with farmers unable to gather enough milk in a single day to make such large cheeses.

The 20th century saw the industrialization of Lancashire, like so many other cheeses, and in 1913 the first dairy producing Lancashire opened in Chipping. During World War II, Lancashire was one of the cheeses banned from production; while 202 farms produced Lancashire in 1939, only 22 continued the tradition by 1948, and the number had dwindled to just seven by 1970.

TYPES OF LANCASHIRE

In Lancashire itself, the cheese is widely eaten in two forms: "Creamy" (a young variety, aged for 4–12 weeks) or "Tasty" (aged for 12–24 weeks). The 1970s saw the development of factory-made "Crumbly" or "New" Lancashire, an acidic, firm-textured cheese made from a single day's curd. Sold very young, New Lancashire offered factories a speedier return than the traditional cheese with its longer maturing period, and today this factory-made version dominates production. The Kirkhams at Goosnargh make a traditional farmhouse variety, while Singletons Dairy has obtained a Protected Designation of Origin (PDO) for its Beacon Fell Traditional Lancashire.

KIRKHAM'S LANCASHIRE

SIZE	
D. 31cm (12¼in)	
H. 23 cm (9in)	
WEIGHT	
20kg (44lb)	
SHAPE Round	
MILK Unpasteurized cow's	
RENNET Traditional animal	
TYPE Traditional	

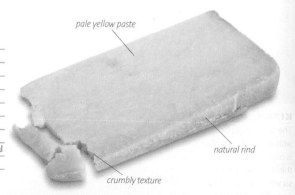

pale yellow paste

natural rind

crumbly texture

KIRKHAM'S LANCASHIRE
The Kirkhams at Goosnargh make this Lancashire with unpasteurized cow's milk and animal rennet. It is produced from the curd of three days' milking, with the clothbound butter-finished cheese matured for six weeks. It has a unique moist yet crumbly texture and a fresh, salty taste with a tang.

LINCOLNSHIRE POACHER
LINCOLNSHIRE

This intriguing mixture between a farmhouse Cheddar and Swiss mountain cheese is made by Simon Jones at Ulceby Grange, Alford. The curd is "Cheddared" and passed through a chip mill. The moulded pressed cheese is matured for 15–20 months. Under the natural rind, the smooth yellow paste has a full, nutty, tasty flavour.

SIZE	
D. 30cm (12in)	
H. 23cm (9in)	
WEIGHT	
20kg (44lb)	
SHAPE Truckle	
MILK Unpasteurized cow's	
RENNET Traditional animal	
TYPE Modern	

LITTLE DERBY WARWICKSHIRE

This cheese is made by Fowlers of Earlswood, makers of Derby cheese since 1940. As the Fowlers had moved to Warwickshire in 1918, the cheese became known as "Little Derby", a name applied to Derby cheese made outside Derbyshire. The cheese is matured for seven months, washed in red wine to create the distinctive orange exterior. The smooth, moist yellow paste has a mild, buttery flavour.

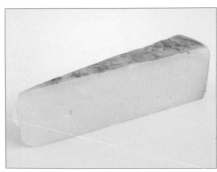

SIZE	
D. 38cm (15in)	
H. 10cm (4in)	
WEIGHT	
11kg (24lb)	
SHAPE Round	
MILK Pasteurized cow's	
RENNET Traditional animal	
TYPE Modern	

LITTLE HEREFORD **HEREFORDSHIRE**

This is made today by Monkland Cheese Dairy following a recipe created for small dairies in the county in 1918 by Ellen Yeld. During the making process, "fingers" of curd are pressed together for three days, creating the characteristic open texture. The cheese is matured for four to five months, during which time it develops a pale golden natural rind. The pale yellow paste has a creamy texture and full, long-lasting flavour.

SIZE	
D. 30cm (12in)	
H. 10cm (4in)	
WEIGHT	
4.5kg (10lb)	
SHAPE Flat cylinder	
MILK Unpasteurized cow's	
RENNET Vegetarian	
TYPE Modern	

LITTLE URN **WORCESTERSHIRE**

Named after England's 2005 Ashes victory over the Australian cricket team, this sheep's cheese is made by Lightwood Cheese. The cut curd is heated, shaped in cloth-lined moulds, dipped in hot water, pressed, and matured for 8–12 months. Little Urn has a golden natural rind and a dry-textured, pale golden paste. The flavour is mild with a lingering nutty sweetness and has a hint of sheep to it.

SIZE	
D. 20cm (8in)	
H. 13cm (5in)	
WEIGHT	
3.8 kg (8½lb)	
SHAPE Cylindrical truckle	
MILK Unpasteurized sheep's	
RENNET Vegetarian	
TYPE Modern	

LLANBOIDY DYFED

Llanboidy Cheesemakers has been making this for 25 years using the milk from its Red Poll cows, but more recently sourcing it from a local co-operative. The curd is cut, blocked, piled, milled, and salted, then packed into moulds and pressed, developing a natural rind. The yellow paste has a smooth, firm texture and a mild flavour when young, developing a tang as it ages.

SIZE	
D. 22cm (8½in)	
H. 8cm (3¼in)	
WEIGHT	
4kg (9lb)	
SHAPE Wheel	
MILK Pasteurized cow's	
RENNET Vegetarian	
TYPE Modern	

LLANGLOFFAN PEMBROKESHIRE

Made originally with unpasteurized cow's milk, this Welsh cheese was created by Leon Downey of Llangloffan Farmhouse Cheese. Today, Carmarthenshire Cheese Company makes it using locally sourced milk. The pressed, moulded cheese is matured for three to four months. It develops a natural rind over a pale yellow paste. Mild and mellow, it is also available smoked, with garlic and chives, and "red" (with annatto).

SIZE	
D. 22cm (8½in)	
H. 7.5cm (3in)	
WEIGHT	
4kg (9lb)	
SHAPE Round	
MILK Unpasteurized cow's	
RENNET Vegetarian	
TYPE Modern	

LOCH ARTHUR DUMFRIES

This is made by the Loch Arthur Community creamery using unpasteurized milk from its cows and local organic herds. It is a clothbound, Cheddar-style cheese, with the curd "Cheddared", milled, pressed, and matured for six months. The matured cheese has a textured rich orange-brown rind, splotched with white mould. The rich golden yellow paste has a smooth texture and full savoury flavour with a tangy sharpness.

SIZE	
D. 24cm (9½in)	
H. 28cm (11in)	
WEIGHT	
8.8–9.5kg (19½–21lb)	
SHAPE Cylinder	
MILK Unpasteurized organic cow's	
RENNET Vegetarian	
TYPE Modern	

LOOSEHANGER WILTSHIRE

Loosehanger Farmhouse Cheeses at Home Farm, Salisbury, makes this cheese using Ayrshire milk supplied from a single herd, grazed on the Hampshire Downs. During the making, the curd is washed and only lightly pressed, before being matured for six to eight weeks. The matured cheese has a dark yellow rind and a moist yellow paste with a scattering of holes. The texture is supple, and the cheese has a mild, mellow flavour.

SIZE	
D. 21cm (8¼in)	
H. 9cm (3½in)	
WEIGHT	
3kg (6½lb)	
SHAPE Round	
MILK Pasteurized cow's	
RENNET Vegetarian	
TYPE Modern	

LORD OF THE HUNDREDS
EAST SUSSEX

This is made by the Traditional Cheese Dairy using unpasteurized sheep's milk. The moulded cheese is brined and matured for four to six months, and it develops a textured golden brown natural rind over a smooth, firm pale paste dotted with holes. It has a dry texture and a mild, nutty flavour with a slight aftertaste of sheep.

SIZE	
D. 18–24cm (7–9½in)	
H. 7.5–11cm (3–4½in)	
WEIGHT	
2.5–4.8kg (5½–10½lb)	
SHAPE Square	
MILK Unpasteurized sheep's	
RENNET Vegetarian	
TYPE Modern	

LYBURN GOLD WILTSHIRE

Lyburn Farmhouse Cheesemakers near Salisbury makes this cheese using pasteurized cow's milk from its own herd. During the making process, the curd is washed, then the moulded cheese is pressed. Lyburn Gold is matured for around 14 weeks, during which time it develops a golden natural rind. The paste is pale yellow, pocked with a few holes, and has a moist, supple texture with a mellow, sweet flavour.

SIZE	
D. 23cm (9in)	
H. 18cm (7in)	
WEIGHT	
4.5kg (10lb)	
SHAPE Round	
MILK Pasteurized cow's	
RENNET Vegetarian	
TYPE Modern	

MAISIE'S KEBBUCK LANARKSHIRE

Humphrey Errington of Walston Braehead created this cheese for Maisie, his mother-in-law, who is not fond of blue cheese, for which Humphrey is especially known. Inspired by the tradition of Scottish farm cheeses before Cheddar techniques, this is an unpressed cheese, matured for three months, with a natural rind. The pale yellow paste has a moist, crumbly texture and a mild, fresh flavour.

SIZE	
D. 22cm (8½in)	
H. 10cm (4in)	
WEIGHT	
3kg (6½lb)	
SHAPE Wheel	
MILK Unpasteurized cow's	
RENNET Vegetarian	
TYPE Modern	

PROTECTING CHEESE VARIETIES

In France, traditionally produced cheeses have long been protected by a legal system known as the *Appellation d'origine contrôlée* (AOC). This system guarantees that a product of quality was produced in a particular region following established methods. In Britain, by contrast, there has been very little protection for traditionally produced cheeses, with Stilton one of the few to have been given guidelines on how and where it can be produced. The name Cheddar, for example, can be used by a factory producer of block-made, plastic-wrapped cheese and by a farmhouse cheesemaker making a traditional, cloth-wrapped Cheddar using milk from the farm's own herd.

Increasingly, cheesemakers are seeking protection through European Union (EU) legislation. The Protected Designation of Origin (PDO) covers foodstuffs produced, processed, and prepared in a given geographical area using recognized expertise, while Protected Geographical Indication (PGI) recognizes a geographical link. Cheeses defined by PDOs include Single Gloucester and Swaledale, while Exmoor Blue has PGI status.

MENALLACK FARMHOUSE
CORNWALL

Menallack Farmhouse at Treverna, Penryn, makes this cheese using unpasteurized cow's milk. The curd is moulded, pressed for three days, then matured for one to three months, depending on the size of the cheese. It develops a brown natural rind over a firm pale yellow paste, and has a mild, mellow taste; there are also flavoured varieties.

SIZE	
D. 11–30cm (4½–12in)	
H. 6–9cm (2½–3½in)	
WEIGHT	
500g–7kg (1lb 2oz–15½lb)	
SHAPE Round	
MILK Unpasteurized cow's	
RENNET Vegetarian	
TYPE Modern	

MILLSTONE SOMERSET

Wootton Organic Dairy makes this cheese using unpasteurized milk from its own sheep. The cheese is unpressed and matured for three to four months, developing a roughly textured, golden brown natural rind, splotched with white mould, over the firm ivory-coloured paste. When young, the flavour is mild; eaten at its peak at around seven to eight months, it has a full salty-sweet flavour and a touch of sharpness.

SIZE	
D. 15–19.5cm (6–7½in)	
H. 7.5–10cm (3–4in)	
WEIGHT	
1.5–2kg (3lb 3oz–4½lb)	
SHAPE Basket	
MILK Unpasteurized organic sheep's	
RENNET Vegetarian	
TYPE Modern	

MONKLAND HEREFORDSHIRE

Made by Monkland Cheese Dairy, this cheese uses a recipe developed by the talented, pioneering cheesemaker James Aldridge. It is an unpressed washed-rind cheese, formed in a flat-bottomed colander which gives it a distinctive shape. Matured for two months, the cheese has an orange rind, coated with white mould, and a moist pale paste with a long-lasting savoury flavour and lemony finish.

SIZE	
D. 15cm (6in)	
H. 7.5cm (3in)	
WEIGHT	
1–2 kg (2¼–4½lb)	
SHAPE Oval	
MILK Unpasteurized cow's	
RENNET Vegetarian	
TYPE Modern	

MOUNT CALLAN CO CLARE

Mount Callan Farmhouse Cheese makes this using unpasteurized milk from the farm's Friesians, only during the summer when the milk is at its richest. Made to a traditional farmhouse Cheddar recipe, it is pressed, clothbound, and matured for 9–18 months, developing a natural rind over a deep yellow paste. The flavour, especially of the longest-matured, is full and powerful with a lingering savouriness.

SIZE	
D. 15cm (6in) & 30cm (12in)	
H. 13cm (5in) & 38cm (15in)	
WEIGHT	
4kg (9lb) & 15kg (33lb)	
SHAPE Truckle	
MILK Unpasteurized cow's	
RENNET Traditional animal	
TYPE Modern	

MR HOLMES'S POMFRIT
YORKSHIRE

Created by cheesemongers Cryer and Stott, this novelty cheese draws on the Yorkshire heritage of liquorice-making. Marinated in a mixture of liquorice liquor and honey, it is a four-week-old Wensleydale-style cheese. It has a dark brown coat over a moist, crumbly white paste with a mild flavour, contrasting with the sweet liquorice taste.

SIZE	
D. 16cm (6½in)	
H. 5cm (2in)	
WEIGHT	
1kg (2¼lb)	
SHAPE Half-moon	
MILK Pasteurized cow's	
RENNET Vegetarian	
TYPE Modern	

MULL OF KINTYRE ARGYLL

The Campbeltown Creamery, housed in a former distillery on the Kintyre peninsula, produces this cheese using pasteurized local cow's milk sourced from within a 10-mile radius. The cheese is made in a large block to a Cheddar recipe for 10–14 months, then cut out from the block and hand-coated with wax. Under the wax coating, the pale yellow paste has a moist texture and a buttery flavour.

SIZE	
D. 8cm (3¼in)	
H. 4cm (1½in)	
WEIGHT	
225g (8oz)	
SHAPE Round	
MILK Pasteurized cow's	
RENNET Vegetarian	
TYPE Modern	

NORFOLK DAPPLE NORFOLK

Ferndale Norfolk Farmhouse Cheese makes this hard-pressed cheese using locally sourced unpasteurized cow's milk. The larger version is made using animal rennet. The curd is moulded, pressed, and matured for three to five months, depending on the size. It develops a golden-brown natural rind over a firm pale yellow paste, and has a mild, mellow flavour. It is also available flavoured with seeds and peppercorns.

SIZE	
D. 10cm (4in) & 20cm (8in)	
H. 9cm (3½in)	
WEIGHT	
4kg (9lb) & 12kg (26½lb)	
SHAPE Round	
MILK Unpasteurized cow's	
RENNET Traditional animal & vegetarian	
TYPE Modern	

NORSWORTHY DEVON

This cheese is made by Norsworthy Dairy in Crediton using unpasteurized milk from the dairy's own herd of goats. The cheese is based on a Dutch recipe, with the curd washed during the making. Matured for a month, it has a golden-brown rind over a white paste with a mild goaty flavour. When milk supplies permit, the dairy matures some Norsworthy for six to seven months, which sees it develop a fuller flavour.

SIZE	
D. 18cm (7in)	
H. 11cm (4½in)	
WEIGHT	
2-2.5kg (4½-5½lb)	
SHAPE Round	
MILK Unpasteurized goat's	
RENNET Vegetarian	
TYPE Modern	

NORTHUMBERLAND
NORTHUMBERLAND

The Northumberland Cheese Company makes this using locally sourced cow's milk from traceable herds. Made in the Gouda style, the curd is scalded, washed, moulded, and brine-bathed, then matured for 12 weeks. It has a smooth, moist texture and mild, creamy flavour. It is also available in flavoured versions.

SIZE	
D. 20cm (9in)	
H. 3cm (7½in)	
WEIGHT	
2–2.5kg (4½–5½lb)	
SHAPE Round	
MILK Pasteurized cow's	
RENNET Vegetarian	
TYPE Modern	

OGLESHIELD SOMERSET

Jamie Montgomery makes this shield-shaped cheese using unpasteurized milk from his Jersey cows. The recipe for this cheese was developed with William Oglethorpe, a fact reflected in the cheese's name. During making, the curd is washed and, as the cheese matures, its rind is brine-washed. Matured for four months, it has a sticky orange rind and a smooth yellow paste with a rich, full, fruity flavour.

SIZE	
D. 32cm (12½in)	
H. 9cm (3½in)	
WEIGHT	
5.5kg (12¼lb)	
SHAPE Disc	
MILK Unpasteurized cow's	
RENNET Traditional animal	
TYPE Modern	

OISIN GOAT CO LIMERICK

Rochus and Rose van der Vaard of Oisin Farmhouse Cheese make this cheese during the spring and summer months using milk from their own goats, which graze the mountain pastures. It is a Gouda-style cheese, reflecting Rochus's Dutch roots, with the curd washed, pressed, and matured for 3–18 months. When young, the white paste is supple and mildly nutty; as it ages, it becomes drier with a fuller flavour.

SIZE	
D. 20cm (8in)	
H. 15cm (6in)	
WEIGHT	
4kg (9lb)	
SHAPE Round	
MILK Pasteurized goat's	
RENNET Vegetarian	
TYPE Modern	

OLD WINCHESTER WILTSHIRE

Lyburn Farmhouse Cheesemakers makes this using unpasteurized milk from its cows. As its name suggests, it is a matured version of Lyburn's Winchester cheese, a hard-pressed cheese, carefully matured until it reaches 16–18 months. It has a deep golden rind and a deep yellow paste with a texture which, while flaky and crumbly, is also moist. The flavour is intensely savoury with a long-lasting salty-sweet finish.

SIZE	
D. 23cm (9in)	
H. 7.5cm (3in)	
WEIGHT	
4kg (9lb)	
SHAPE Round	
MILK Unpasteurized cow's	
RENNET Vegetarian	
TYPE Modern	

OLD WORCESTER WHITE
WORCESTERSHIRE

Named after the county in which it is made, this hard cheese is produced by Ansteys at Broomhall Farm. During making, the curd is cut into small blocks, which are moulded and pressed. Matured for six months, it develops a brown natural rind, blotched with white mould, and a firm pale yellow paste. The flavour is subtle with a milky nuttiness.

SIZE	
D. 20cm (8in)	
H. 15cm (6in)	
WEIGHT	
3.5kg (7½lb)	
SHAPE Round	
MILK Pasteurized cow's	
RENNET Vegetarian	
TYPE Modern	

OLDE GLOSTER   GLOUCESTERSHIRE

This clothbound hard cheese, based on a Double Gloucester recipe, is made by Lightwood Cheese using unpasteurized cow's milk. In order to retain more moisture in the cheese, the curd is scalded at a lower heat and not cut too small. Carrot juice and annatto are added for colour and flavour. Matured for seven months, the cheese has a dark orange rind, bright orange paste, and a full, sweet taste with an after-tang.

SIZE	
D. 20cm (8in)	
H. 13cm (5in)	
WEIGHT	
6.8kg (15lb)	
SHAPE Cylindrical truckle	
MILK Unpasteurized cow's	
RENNET Vegetarian	
TYPE Modern	

OLDE SUSSEX EAST SUSSEX

The Traditional Cheese Dairy at Wadhurst makes this hard cheese using unpasteurized cow's milk sourced from local farms and dairies. The curd is cut, drained, moulded, pressed, and matured for three to four months, during which time it develops a natural rind, coated with white mould. The smooth yellow paste has a moist, open texture, and the flavour is mild with a sweet nuttiness to it.

SIZE
D. 24cm (9½in)
H. 7.5cm (3in)
WEIGHT
4.3kg (9½lb)
SHAPE Cylinder
MILK Unpasteurized cow's
RENNET Vegetarian
TYPE Modern

ORKNEY ORKNEY ISLANDS

Hilda Seator at Grimbister Farm on the Isle of Orkney makes this Scottish cheese using unpasteurized milk from the farm's own herd of Friesian cows. The milk from the farm is curdled, then the curd is drained, cut, moulded, and pressed for a day, with the cheese sold while it is still very young. The pale paste has a very crumbly, moist texture, while the flavour is fresh and lactic with a faint citrus kick.

SIZE
D. 13–18cm (5–7in)
H. 6–15cm (2½–6in)
WEIGHT
700g–3.5kg (1¾–7½lb)
SHAPE Truckle
MILK Unpasteurized cow's
RENNET Vegetarian
TYPE Modern

PENDRAGON SOMERSET

One of a handful of British cheeses that uses buffalo's milk, this is made by the Somerset Cheese Company at Ditcheat Hill Farm. The curds are moulded, pressed overnight, and matured for between 4–12 months. During this time, Pendragon develops a brown natural rind and a firm yellow paste with a creamy texture, due to the milk's fat content, and a mild, sweet flavour.

SIZE
D. 18cm (7in) & 25cm (10in)
H. 7cm (2¾in)
WEIGHT
2kg (4½lb) & 3.5kg (7½lb)
SHAPE Round
MILK Pasteurized buffalo's
RENNET Vegetarian
TYPE Modern

PENNARD RIDGE SOMERSET

This flaky-textured goat's cheese is made by the Somerset Cheese Company at Ditcheat Hill Farm, and named after the local ridge. Made in the Caerphilly style, the cheese is pressed, then brine-washed for a day, and matured for 8–10 weeks. It has a golden-brown natural rind, dusted with white mould, and an open-textured white paste with a nutty-sweet taste that has a hint of goat.

SIZE
D. 18cm (7in) & 25cm (10in)
H. 7cm (2¾in)
WEIGHT
2kg (4½lb) & 3.5kg (7½lb)
SHAPE Wheel
MILK Pasteurized goat's
RENNET Vegetarian
TYPE Modern

PENNARD RIDGE RED SOMERSET

The Somerset Cheese Company makes this "goat Red Leicester" at Ditcheat Hill Farm using locally sourced milk. To create a more open-textured cheese, Philip Rainbow scalds the curd at a lower heat than is used for Cheddar and works the curd less. Matured for 4–12 months, it has a brown natural rind, while annatto gives the cheese its distinctive deep orange colour. The flavour is nutty-sweet with a touch of goat.

SIZE	
D. 18cm (7in) & 25cm (10in)	
H. 7cm (2¾in)	
WEIGHT	
2kg (4½lb) & 3.5kg (7½lb)	
SHAPE	Wheel
MILK	Pasteurized goat's
RENNET	Vegetarian
TYPE	Modern

PENNARD VALE SOMERSET

This hard goat's cheese is made by The Somerset Cheese Company at Ditcheat Hill Farm using locally sourced goat's milk. The curd is moulded, pressed overnight, and matured for between 4–12 months. During this time, it develops a brown natural rind, evenly dusted with white mould, while the waxy-textured paste is white and smooth. The flavour is salty-sweet and nutty with a tang of goat to it.

SIZE	
D. 18cm (7in) & 25cm (10in)	
H. 7cm (2¾in)	
WEIGHT	
2kg (4½lb) & 3.5kg (7½lb)	
SHAPE	Wheel
MILK	Pasteurized goat's
RENNET	Vegetarian
TYPE	Modern

QUICKE'S HARD GOAT DEVON

This is made by Quickes Traditional at Home Farm, Newton St Cyres, using goat's milk sourced from Devon and Dorset. It is made along similar lines to the Cheddar that Quickes also makes, with the curd scalded, "Cheddared", milled, salted, moulded, wrapped in cheesecloth, and matured for 6–10 months. The cheese develops a natural rind over a firm white paste with a sweet nuttiness of flavour.

SIZE	
D. 35.5cm (14in)	
H. 30cm (12in)	
WEIGHT	
24kg (53lb)	
SHAPE Truckle	
MILK Pasteurized goat's	
RENNET Vegetarian	
TYPE Modern	

RED LEICESTER LEICESTERSHIRE

Leicestershire Handmade Cheese Company at Sparkenhoe Farm has revived the making of this traditional cheese in the county in which it originated. It is made with unpasteurized milk from the farm's cows, coloured with annatto to give the paste the traditional deep orange colour associated with the cheese. Matured for between three to six months, the clothbound cheese has a firm texture and gentle lactic flavour.

SIZE	
D. 35.5cm (14in) & 46cm (18in)	
H. 13cm (5in) & 18cm (7in)	
WEIGHT	
10kg (22lb) & 20kg (44lb)	
SHAPE Wheel	
MILK Unpasteurized cow's	
RENNET Traditional animal	
TYPE Traditional	

REIVER NORTHUMBERLAND

The Northumberland Cheese Company at Blagdon makes this cheese using pasteurized cow's milk. To create the white-mould layer, *Penicillium candidum* is added to the milk at the beginning of the process. The cheese is moulded and pressed, and matured for 10–12 weeks, developing a bumpy natural rind coated in bloomy white mould. The moist yellow paste has a mild flavour with a mushroomy note.

SIZE	
D. 20cm (8in)	
H. 7.5cm (3in)	
WEIGHT	
2–2.5kg (4½–5½lb)	
SHAPE Round	
MILK Pasteurized cow's	
RENNET Vegetarian	
TYPE Modern	

RIBBLESDALE ORIGINAL
NORTH YORKSHIRE

A hard goat's cheese made for the Ribblesdale Cheese Company, Horton-in-Ribblesdale, this follows a recipe from its founder, the late Iain Hill. The cheese is aged for two to three months and is coated with a pale wax covering. The firm bright white paste has a crumbly texture and a lactic taste with only a hint of goat.

SIZE	
D. 20cm (8in)	
H. 6cm (2½in)	
WEIGHT	
2kg (4½lb)	
SHAPE Wheel	
MILK Pasteurized goat's	
RENNET Vegetarian	
TYPE Modern	

RINGWELL SOMERSET

Wootton Organic Dairy makes this cheese using locally sourced organic milk from a Jersey herd. An unpressed cheese, it is moulded in colanders, giving it a distinctive shape, and matured for at least three to four months. The rough natural rind covers a rich golden yellow paste dotted with holes. The texture is firm but moist, and the cheese has a mild but full flavour with a creamy sweetness to the taste.

SIZE	
D. 15–19.5cm (6–7½in)	
H. 7.5–10cm (3–4in)	
WEIGHT	
1.5–2kg (3lb 3oz–4½lb)	
SHAPE Basket	
MILK Unpasteurized organic cow's	
RENNET Vegetarian	
TYPE Modern	

SHEEP'S MILK WENSLEYDALE
YORKSHIRE

The Wensleydale Creamery makes this version of its classic Wensleydale using locally sourced sheep's milk, in a revival of the ancient tradition started by Cistercian monks, who first brought cheese-making to Yorkshire. The gleaming white paste of this Wensleydale is soft and moist, while the flavour is fresh and mild.

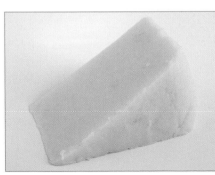

SIZE	
D. 7cm (2¾in)	
H. 10cm (4in)	
WEIGHT	
1.1kg (2½lb)	
SHAPE Cylinder	
MILK Pasteurized sheep's	
RENNET Vegetarian	
TYPE Traditional	

SHIPCORD SUFFOLK

This hard cow's cheese is made by Rodwell Farm Dairy at its farm in Baylham. The unpasteurized cow's milk is curdled, and the curd is very finely chopped and the whey thoroughly drained off. The pressed, moulded cheese is matured for six months and develops a pale brown natural rind over a firm yellow paste with a smooth texture. The flavour is mild, but with a butterscotch sweetness to it.

SIZE	
D. 25cm (10in)	
H. 10cm (4in)	
WEIGHT	
4.3–4.8kg (9½–10½lb)	
SHAPE Round	
MILK Unpasteurized cow's	
RENNET Vegetarian	
TYPE Modern	

TOOLS OF THE TRADE

As in any specialist area of production, cheesemakers use specific tools. Several of these are traditional ones, little changed in function or design for centuries.

• **Curd knives:** these are used to cut the set curd, releasing the whey. The term is applied to long-bladed fine knives, but also to wire-strung cutters, sometimes called "cheese harps", which can be passed through the vat to cube the curd.

• **Cheese press:** To make a hard-pressed cheese, the curd is placed in a mould and pressed in a press, with the cheesemaker varying the pressure as required.

• **Cheese iron:** this is used to check the progress of a large hard cheese without cutting it. The sample is pulled out, then pushed back in to plug the hole once the cheese has been assessed.

CHEESE IRON
The iron is used to pull out a plug of cheese so that it can be checked.

SINGLE GLOUCESTER
GLOUCESTERSHIRE

Charles Martell revived the making of Single Gloucester, which now has a Protected Designation of Origin (PDO), meaning it can be made only in Gloucestershire on farms with a pedigree herd of Old Gloucesters. Matured for two to three months, it has a pale paste under a mouldy natural rind with a soft, creamy texture and mild lactic flavour.

SIZE	
D. 22cm (8½in)	
H. 7cm (2¾in)	
WEIGHT	
2.25kg (5lb)	
SHAPE Wheel	
MILK Pasteurized cow's	
RENNET Vegetarian	
TYPE Traditional	

SNODSBURY GOAT
WORCESTERSHIRE

Made by Ansteys using unpasteurized goat's milk, the curd is pressed for 48 hours and the clothbound cheeses matured for four months. It has a very pale brown natural rind, blotched with white mould, and a firm-textured white to ivory-coloured paste. The flavour is goaty, but not overpowering, and it has a rich, full nuttiness.

SIZE	
D. 20cm (8in)	
H. 10cm (4in)	
WEIGHT	
1.8 kg (4lb)	
SHAPE Wheel	
MILK Unpasteurized goat's	
RENNET Vegetarian	
TYPE Modern	

SPENWOOD **BERKSHIRE**

Village Maid makes this unpasteurized sheep's milk cheese named after Spencers Wood Village. The drained, moulded cheese is matured for six months, in which time it develops a brown natural rind over a gleaming paste. The texture is slightly flaky, while the flavour is nutty with a lingering sweetness. As it matures, the texture of Spenwood becomes harder and drier, and the flavour, spicier and fuller.

SIZE	
D. 20cm (8in)	
H. 7.5cm (3in)	
WEIGHT	
2kg (4½lb)	
SHAPE Round	
MILK Unpasteurized sheep's	
RENNET Vegetarian	
TYPE Modern	

ST EGWIN **WORCESTERSHIRE**

This cheese is made by Gorsehill Abbey Cheese using organic milk from its own herd of Friesian and Montbeliarde cows at Gorsehill Abbey Farm. Named after the founder of the local Evesham Abbey, St Egwin is matured for one to eight months, developing a white-dusted golden rind over a deep yellow paste pocked with holes. The texture is moist and pliable, and it has a mild but lingering nutty sweetness.

SIZE	
D. 20cm (8in)	
H. 11cm (4½in)	
WEIGHT	
2.25kg (5lb)	
SHAPE Low cylinder	
MILK Pasteurized cow's	
RENNET Animal	
TYPE Modern	

ST GALL CO CORK

This Irish cheese is made by the Fermoy Cheese Company using milk from its own Friesians. The curd is heated in copper-lined vats, cut very finely, pressed, brine-bathed, and matured on timber boards, smeared with a brine solution. Matured for five to six months, it has a golden-orange rind, a spicy aroma, and a smooth deep yellow paste, dotted with tiny bubbles. The flavour is rich, mellow, and lingering.

SIZE	
D. 30cm (12in)	
H. 10cm (4in)	
WEIGHT	
4.8kg (10½lb)	
SHAPE Wheel	
MILK Unpasteurized cow's	
RENNET Traditional animal	
TYPE Modern	

ST KENELM WORCESTERSHIRE

Gorsehill Abbey Cheese at Gorsehill Abbey Farm makes this cheese, named after an ancient king of Mercia, using organic milk from its own cows. The cheese is matured for two to six months, developing a natural rind over the rich yellow paste. The texture is firm but moist with a creaminess to it and a mild flavour, although as the cheese matures this takes on more of a tang.

SIZE	
D. 20cm (8in)	
H. 11cm (4½in)	
WEIGHT	
2.25kg (5lb)	
SHAPE Low cylinder	
MILK Pasteurized cow's	
RENNET Traditional animal	
TYPE Modern	

SUSSEX SCRUMPY EAST SUSSEX

The Traditional Cheese Dairy at Wadhurst makes this cheese using unpasteurized milk sourced from local farms and dairies. Made in the Cheddar style, a mixture of cider, herbs, and garlic is added to the paste and the cheese is matured for three months. The creamy-textured pale yellow paste is flecked with green, and the cheese has a savoury, garlicky flavour with the sweetness of the cider also noticeable.

SIZE	
D. 24cm (9½in)	
H. 7.5cm (3in)	
WEIGHT	
2kg (4½lb)	
SHAPE Half-moon	
MILK Pasteurized cow's	
RENNET Vegetarian	
TYPE Modern	

SUSSEX YEOMAN EAST SUSSEX

Nut Knowle Farm at Horam makes this hard-pressed cheese using pasteurized milk from its herd of Toggenburg and British Saanen goats. The curd is finely cut, scalded, moulded, pressed, and brined, then matured for two months. During maturation, it develops a textured, golden-brown natural rind over a white paste, which has a slightly moist and crumbly texture. The flavour is mild and nutty-sweet.

SIZE	
D. 18cm (7in)	
H. 9cm (3½in)	
WEIGHT	
2kg (4½lb)	
SHAPE Wheel	
MILK Pasteurized goat's	
RENNET Vegetarian	
TYPE Modern	

SWALEDALE GOAT YORKSHIRE

Swaledale cheese has traditionally been made in the Yorkshire Dales for centuries, with this hard goat's cheese being made by the Swaledale Cheese Company. The goat's milk curd is milled, moulded, pressed, bathed in brine overnight, and matured for six weeks, during which time it is brushed and turned. It has a grey-brown natural rind and a firm white paste, which has a salty-sweet, goaty flavour.

SIZE	
D. 16cm (6½in)	
H. 8cm (3¼in)	
WEIGHT	
2.5kg (5½lb)	
SHAPE	Round
MILK	Pasteurized goat's
RENNET	Vegetarian
TYPE	Modern

SWEET CHARLOTTE DEVON

This hard cheese is made for Country Cheeses by Rachel Stephens of Curworthy Cheeses using milk from her own herd of Friesians and a starter culture used for Jarlsberg and Emmenthal cheeses. Matured for six to eight months, the cheese develops a rich golden rind over a yellow paste dotted with tiny holes. The texture is smooth and slippery, while the flavour is rich and full with a long-lasting finish.

SIZE	
D. 18cm (7in)	
H. 9cm (3½in)	
WEIGHT	
3kg (6½lb)	
SHAPE	Round
MILK	Pasteurized cow's
RENNET	Vegetarian
TYPE	Modern

TEIFI CEREDIGION

John Savage of Teifi Farmhouse Cheese makes this cheese using unpasteurized cow's milk from a single herd. The cheese is matured for 12 weeks–2 years, depending on size. It has a golden rind and a smooth yellow paste. When young, Teifi is sweet and buttery; when aged, it becomes drier and flakier with a stronger taste. It is available in flavoured versions, including cumin, a nod to John's Dutch ancestry.

SIZE	
D. 10–40cm (4–16in)	
H. 6–15cm (2½–6in)	
WEIGHT	
500g–12kg (1lb 2oz–26½lb)	
SHAPE Wheel	
MILK Unpasteurized cow's	
RENNET Vegetarian	
TYPE Modern	

TICKLEMORE DEVON

Ticklemore cheese was originally created and made by cheesemaker Robin Congdon of Ticklemore Cheeses. Nowadays, however, the cheese is made on the Sharpham Estate by Debbie Mumford, who used to work with Robin. The cheese has a textured rind from the baskets in which it is formed and a fine white paste, dotted with holes. The paste is moist and crumbly, and has a subtle, fresh flavour.

SIZE	
D. 18cm (7in)	
H. 8cm (3¼in)	
WEIGHT	
1.5kg (3lb 3oz)	
SHAPE Basket	
MILK Pasteurized goat's	
RENNET Vegetarian	
TYPE Modern	

TREHILL DEVON

This flavoured cheese is made for Country Cheeses by Rachel Stephens using milk from her herd of Friesian cows. Garlic and chives are added to the curd, which is then moulded, pressed, and brined. It is matured for three to four months. A dark green wax coating covers a moist yellow paste flecked with dark green flakes, and the texture is creamy with the garlic and chives flavour dominating the cheese.

SIZE	
D. 9cm (3 ½in) & 19.5cm (7½in)	
H. 5cm (2in) & 7.5cm (3in)	
WEIGHT	
400g (14oz) & 2.2kg (5lb)	
SHAPE Round	
MILK Pasteurized cow's	
RENNET Vegetarian	
TYPE Modern	

TRELAWNY CORNWALL

Whalesborough Farm Foods near Bude makes this hard cheese from pasteurized cow's milk. The moulded curd is pressed for 24 hours, and the cheese is matured for six to eight weeks, during which time it develops a grey-brown natural rind, splotched with pink mould from the dairy in which it is made. The pale yellow paste has a firm texture and a balanced yet lingering flavour.

SIZE	
D. 20cm (8in)	
H. 10cm (4in)	
WEIGHT	
1.5kg (3lb 3oz)	
SHAPE Wheel	
MILK Pasteurized cow's	
RENNET Vegetarian	
TYPE Modern	

CLOTHBOUND CHEESES

A characteristic of traditional British cheese-making is the practice of wrapping cheese in muslin, so that it is protected but allowed to breathe as it matures.

TREMAINS SUSSEX

High Weald Dairy in Horsted Keynes make this organic Cheddar cheese, named after the farm where the cheese is made. To make the cheese, the curd is cut, milled, moulded, and pressed, then set aside to mature for at least three months. The matured cheese has a golden natural rind and a pale yellow paste with a smooth, creamy texture and a full flavour with a tang to it.

SIZE	
D. 24cm (9.5in)	
H. 7–8cm (2¾–3¼in)	
WEIGHT	
3kg (6½lb)	
SHAPE Round	
MILK Pasteurized organic cow's	
RENNET Vegetarian	
TYPE Modern	

VILLAGE GREEN CORNWALL

Cornish Country Larder makes this hard goat's cheese at its creamery near Padstow in Cornwall, using goat's milk sourced from a number of farms that supply the creamery. The cheese is matured for six months and is coated in a bright green wax covering, contrasting with the bright white interior. The paste is crumbly and moist, and the cheese has a mild flavour with only a hint of goat to it.

SIZE	
D. 9cm (3½in)	
H. 7cm (2¾in)	
WEIGHT	
1.25kg (2¾lb)	
SHAPE Block	
MILK Pasteurized goat's	
RENNET Vegetarian	
TYPE Modern	

WARWICKSHIRE TRUCKLE
WEST MIDLANDS

Fowlers of Earlswood has been making this cheese for more than 70 years. The scalded curd is milled, moulded, and pressed, before being clothbound and waxed. Matured for seven months, it has a firm, moist yellow paste with a mild flavour. It is available in flavoured versions layered with garlic and parsley, chilli, or black pepper.

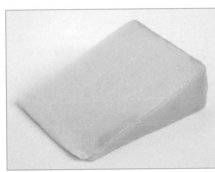

SIZE	
D. 20cm (8in)	
H. 20cm (8in)	
WEIGHT	
6kg (13lb)	
SHAPE Truckle	
MILK Pasteurized cow's	
RENNET Vegetarian	
TYPE Traditional	

WEDMORE SOMERSET

Duckett's, best known for its Caerphilly, makes this cheese at Westcombe Dairy, near Shepton Mallet. While the curd is being placed in the moulds, a layer of chopped chives is added. Matured for only two weeks, the cheese does not develop a rind. It is a pale cream-coloured cheese, marked with a band of green, with a crumbly, moist texture. The salty mildness of the cheese contrasts with the onion flavour of chives.

SIZE	
D. 17cm (6¾in)	
H. 7.5cm (3in)	
WEIGHT	
2kg (4½lb)	
SHAPE Wheel	
MILK Pasteurized cow's	
RENNET Vegetarian	
TYPE Modern	

WENSLEYDALE YORKSHIRE

A HISTORIC YORKSHIRE CHEESE, Wensleydale originated with French Cistercian monks from the Roquefort region who came to England with William the Conqueror. The monks settled in the Yorkshire Dales, building first a monastery at Fors in 1150AD, then an abbey at Jervaulx in Lower Wensleydale. The monks made cheese from the local ewes' milk, and used mould from local stone to create a blue version. Their knowledge spread to the surrounding populace, and even after the monasteries were dissolved under Henry VIII the monks' traditional cheese continued to thrive. The use of the name "Wensleydale" for the cheese has been traced back to 1840, when grocers could buy a soft-textured, moist blue-veined cheese at annual cheese fairs.

PRODUCING WENSLEYDALE

By the mid-17th century, cow's milk had replaced sheep's in most British cheeses, and Wensleydale was no exception. In the late 19th century, Edward Chapman, a provision merchant and major buyer of farmhouse Wensleydale, set up a Wensleydale Cheese Factory, making a white cheese with a firmer texture than the traditional farmhouse variety. During World War II, the Ministry of Food ordered that only Chapman's harder, longer-lasting version could be produced, and farmhouse Wensleydale largely disappeared.

Today, Wensleydale Dairy Products at Hawes Creamery is the only company that continues to make the cheese in Wensleydale itself. Classic Wensleydale has a pale white paste, a distinctive flaky, moist texture, and a delicate sweetness of flavour. In Yorkshire, Wensleydale is often eaten with sweet foods such as fruit cake.

HAWES'S WENSLEYDALE

SIZE	
D. 18cm (7in)	
H. 18cm (7in)	
WEIGHT	
5kg (11lb)	
SHAPE	Truckle
MILK	Pasteurized cow's
RENNET	Traditional animal or vegetarian
TYPE	Traditional

flaky and moist

cream-coloured paste

HAWES'S WENSLEYDALE

Hawes Creamery in Wensleydale makes this cheese
using locally sourced cow's milk. To create the
characteristic flaky, moist texture, the cheese is only
lightly pressed. Matured for four to six months, it has
a cream-coloured paste and a delicate taste. It is also
available in flavoured versions.

WHITE STILTON NOTTINGHAMSHIRE

White Stilton, though made by Stilton makers, is an unveined cheese, with no *Penicillium roqueforti* added to the milk or piercing of the cheese during maturing. An unpressed cheese, this white Stilton is made by Cropwell Bishop Creamery, sold while very young. The pale paste is crumbly and moist, with a fresh, mild flavour. It is available in a number of flavoured versions, including cranberry and blueberry.

SIZE	
D. 20cm (8in)	
H. 25cm (10in)	
WEIGHT	
8kg (17½lb)	
SHAPE	Cylinder
MILK	Pasteurized cow's
RENNET	Vegetarian
TYPE	Modern

WILD GARLIC YARG CORNWALL

Lynher Dairy at Pengreep Farm makes this flavoured cheese using cow's milk from the dairy's own herd and neighbouring farms. The moulded cheeses are brine-washed overnight, dried, then covered with wild garlic leaves. As the cheese matures, a sprinkling of white mould grows on the green leaf wrapping. Once ready to eat, it has a moist, creamy-textured white paste with a mild garlic flavour.

SIZE	
D. 19cm (7¼in)	
H. 7cm (2¾in)	
WEIGHT	
1.7kg (3¾lb)	
SHAPE	Wheel
MILK	Pasteurized cow's
RENNET	Vegetarian
TYPE	Modern

WOOLSERY ENGLISH GOAT

DORSET

Woolsery Cheese makes this cheese using Dorset-sourced pasteurized goat's milk. The curd is drained, moulded, and pressed in Victorian cheese presses, then matured for 8–12 weeks. It develops a brown natural rind over a smooth white paste. The texture is firm, yet moist, and it has a salty-nutty taste with only a hint of goat.

SIZE	
D. 6cm (2½in)	
H. 6cm (2½in)	
WEIGHT	
2.2kg (5lb)	
SHAPE Round	
MILK Pasteurized goat's	
RENNET Vegetarian	
TYPE Modern	

THE BRITISH CHEESE AWARDS

In 1994 Juliet Harbutt, a noted cheese expert, established the British Cheese Awards with the aims of raising the standards of British cheese and creating a symbol of excellence. In 1994, its inaugural year, 97 cheesemakers entered fewer than 300 cheeses. By 2007, 175 cheesemakers submitted almost 900 cheeses, proving how much the event had grown. Cheeses are submitted within a large variety of categories, including by type (such as blue, fresh, soft), "Best Organic", and other categories, such as "Best Scottish". The cheeses are judged in the summer by a panel from around the world, and the winners are announced at the autumn Awards Dinner. There are winners in each category and one overall Supreme Champion. Winning an award here is a source of great pride for cheesemakers.

Juliet runs other events to promote British cheeses: The Great British Cheese Festival is designed to inform the public about the wide variety of British cheeses, and British Cheese Week promotes British cheese in shops and restaurants.

WORCESTERSHIRE SAUCE
WORCESTERSHIRE

Made by Ansteys, this cheese is characterized by the addition of a classic British condiment, Worcestershire sauce, made by nearby Lea & Perrins. Matured for only three months, it has a golden natural rind, with white mould, and a pale yellow paste with distinctive purple-brown marbling. The flavour is subtly spicy with a hint of pickles.

SIZE	
D. 20cm (8in)	
H. 15cm (6in)	
WEIGHT	
3.5kg (7½lb)	
SHAPE Round	
MILK Pasteurized cow's	
RENNET Vegetarian	
TYPE Modern	

WYFE OF BATH SOMERSET

Named after Chaucer's pilgrim, this is made by Bath Soft Cheese at Park Farm, Kelston, using milk from the farm's own cows. The cheese is made from unpressed washed curd, then moulded in baskets and drained under its own weight. Matured for 10 weeks, it develops a golden natural rind, flecked with white mould. The pale yellow paste has a little bounce to it, and the flavour is mild yet full.

SIZE	
D. 25cm (10in)	
H. 38cm (15in)	
WEIGHT	
3kg (6½lb)	
SHAPE Basket	
MILK Pasteurized cow's	
RENNET Vegetarian	
TYPE Modern	

Y-FENNI GWENT

This flavoured cheese is produced by Abergavenny Fine Foods and is named after the Welsh name for Abergavenny, the town in which it is made. The cheese is made by blending mature Cheddar cheese with whole-grain mustard and Welsh ale. The mixture is then moulded and coated in wax. The yellow paste, speckled with mustard seeds, has a moist texture and a savoury, mildly piquant flavour.

SIZE	
D. 18cm (7in)	
H. 5cm (2in)	
WEIGHT	
1.5kg (3lb 3oz)	
SHAPE Wheel	
MILK Pasteurized cow's	
RENNET Vegetarian	
TYPE Modern	

THE PASTEURIZATION DEBATE

Today, the majority of cheese is made from pasteurized milk, which has been heat-treated – usually to a temperature of 71.7°C (161°F) for 15 seconds – to kill micro-organisms that cause disease and decay. The technique was invented by Louis Pasteur in 1862, and for hundreds of years prior to that all cheese was made with untreated milk. Pasteurization has gone hand in hand with the industrialization of cheese-making, enabling dairies to transport milk from farms to factories without it souring.

Many cheesemakers and cheesemongers passionately believe that cheese should be made from raw milk. Pasteurization, they point out, kills not just pathogenic (disease-causing) bacteria, but also harmless micro-organisms that enhance the flavour of cheese. Heat-treated milk tends to be uniform and lacks the depth of flavour found in "raw" milk; it consequently produces less interesting cheese with no sense of place. Health concerns, they argue, are exaggerated: many cheese-related food scares have involved cheese made from pasteurized rather than raw milk, and poor hygiene in the dairy or during maturing poses a much greater threat than natural milk bacteria.

BLUE CHEESES

Easily identified by the veins of blue-green mould that run through them, blue cheeses have a fairly soft texture and a distinctive tang, resulting from the development of mould within the cheese. Stilton is Britain's best-known blue cheese, tracing its history back to the 18th century, but several other notable blues are well worth sampling.

BADENTOY BLUE ABERDEENSHIRE

Devenick Dairy near Aberdeen makes this cheese using pasteurized milk from its herd of dairy cows. *Penicillium roqueforti* is added to the milk at the beginning of the cheese-making process to ensure the development of the veining, and the moulded cheese is pierced. Matured for four months, it develops a natural rind over a firm, moist yellow paste with scattered veining. The flavour is only mildly blue.

SIZE	
D. 14.5cm (5¾in)	
H. 8cm (3¼in)	
WEIGHT	
1.3kg (3lb)	
SHAPE Round	
MILK Pasteurized cow's	
RENNET Vegetarian	
TYPE Modern	

BARKHAM BLUE BERKSHIRE

Two Hoots Cheese in Barkham makes this blue cheese using pasteurized Channel Islands' milk, with its high butterfat content. *Penicillium roqueforti* is added to the milk, with the unpressed, moulded cheese pierced at a week old to encourage veining. Matured for five to six weeks, it has a pale yellow paste and blue-green veining. There is a buttery texture and sweet flavour, and a savoury note from the veining.

SIZE	
D. 18cm (7in)	
H. 7.5cm (3in)	
WEIGHT	
1.3kg (3lb)	
SHAPE Round	
MILK Pasteurized cow's	
RENNET Vegetarian	
TYPE Modern	

BEENLEIGH BLUE DEVON

Ticklemore Cheeses near Sharpham Barton, pioneer makers of blue sheep's milk cheeses, makes Beenleigh Blue. This unpressed cheese is foil-wrapped once the blue has developed sufficiently, and matured until it is at least five months old. The resulting cheese has a pale paste streaked with blue-green veining. With a crumbly, moist texture and sweet, complex flavour, it has a savouriness from the veining.

SIZE	
D. 20cm (8in)	
H. 10–13cm (4–5in)	
WEIGHT	
3–3½kg (6½–7½lb)	
SHAPE Round	
MILK Pasteurized sheep's	
RENNET Vegetarian	
TYPE Modern	

BELLINGHAM BLUE CO LOUTH

Peter Thomas of Glyde Farm Produce, Castlebellingham, makes this Irish blue cheese using unpasteurized cow's milk from his brother-in-law's herd of Friesians. The unpressed cheese is hand-pierced at two weeks, then ripened for four months. Once matured, it has a pale golden natural rind and a moist cream-coloured paste dotted with blue-green mould, and a rich, full, nutty lingering flavour.

SIZE	
D. 20cm (8in)	
H. 7.5–11cm (3–4½in)	
WEIGHT	
3–4kg (6½–9lb)	
SHAPE Round	
MILK Unpasteurized cow's	
RENNET Vegetarian	
TYPE Modern	

BIRDWOOD BLUE HEAVEN
GLOUCESTERSHIRE

Made by Birdwood Farmhouse Cheesemakers, this cheese uses unpasteurized milk from a herd of Shorthorns. *Penicillium roqueforti* is added, and it is matured for at least four weeks, developing a natural crust over a pale yellow paste, blotched with mould. The texture is creamy and yielding, while the flavour has a marked piquancy.

SIZE	
D. 5cm (2in) & 20cm (8in)	
H. 5cm (2in) & 15cm (6in)	
WEIGHT	
400g (14oz) & 1.5kg (3lb 3oz)	
SHAPE	Round
MILK	Unpasteurized cow's
RENNET	Vegetarian
TYPE	Modern

BLACKSTICKS BLUE LANCASHIRE

Blacksticks Blue is made by Butlers Farmhouse Cheese, near Preston, using milk from the farm's herd. To give the cheese its striking bright orange colour, annatto is added to the milk, while *Penicillium roqueforti* is used to create the blue-green moulding. Once moulded, the cheese is pierced to encourage the veining, and it is matured for two months. The soft orange paste has a creamy texture and a buttery tang.

SIZE	
D. 21cm (8¼in)	
H. 6cm (2½in)	
WEIGHT	
2.5kg (5½lb)	
SHAPE	Cylinder
MILK	Pasteurized cow's
RENNET	Vegetarian
TYPE	Modern

BLISSFUL BUFFALO SOMERSET

One of the few British buffalo's milk blue cheeses, this is made by the Exmoor Blue Cheese Company at Willett Farm, Lydeard St Lawrence. The cheese is matured for four to six weeks, during which time it develops a golden-brown natural rind over an ivory-coloured paste, lightly veined with green-blue mould. The texture is dense and moist, with the milky sweetness of the milk contrasting with the tang of the mould.

SIZE	
D. 13cm (5in)	
H. 9cm (3½in)	
WEIGHT	
1kg (2¼lb)	
SHAPE Cylinder	
MILK Unpasteurized buffalo's	
RENNET Vegetarian	
TYPE Modern	

BLUE CHESHIRE CHESHIRE

H.S. Bourne, whose family has been making Cheshire cheese for generations, makes this traditional cheese using milk from his own cows. It is pressed, pierced, and matured for six to seven months in an old cellar, where the mould in the atmosphere penetrates the cheese. The mature cheese has a natural rind and a flaky, moist paste splotched with blue. The flavour is mild with a gentle spiciness from the blue veining.

SIZE	
D. 23cm (9in)	
H. 23cm (9in)	
WEIGHT	
8kg (17½lb)	
SHAPE Round	
MILK Pasteurized cow's	
RENNET Vegetarian	
TYPE Traditional	

BLUE HILLS SOMERSET

This blue cheese is made for Country Cheeses by cheesemaker Ian Arnett of Exmoor Blue Cheese. Unusually, it is made with a mixture of both cow's and goat's milks. Matured for two months, the cheese develops a distinctive dark brown-grey rind, coating a pale paste with only a touch of barely visible veining. It has a firm but moist texture and a full flavour with a tangy finish due to the goat's milk.

SIZE	
D. 13cm (5in)	
H. 10cm (4in)	
WEIGHT	
1kg (2¼lb)	
SHAPE Round	
MILK Unpasteurized cow's & goat's	
RENNET Vegetarian	
TYPE Modern	

BLUE WENSLEYDALE YORKSHIRE

The Wensleydale Creamery makes this cheese from locally sourced cow's milk, reviving a tradition of making a blue Wensleydale. To create the blueing, *Penicillium roqueforti* is added, and the moulded curd is lightly pressed, with the cheese pierced later on to encourage the veining. Matured for six months, it develops a natural rind over a firm pale paste mottled with veining. The flavour is mellow and savoury.

SIZE	
D. 17.5cm (6¾in)	
H. 19.5cm (7½in)	
WEIGHT	
5kg (11lb)	
SHAPE Round	
MILK Pasteurized cow's	
RENNET Vegetarian	
TYPE Traditional	

BLUE WHINNOW CUMBRIA

Thornby Dairy at Crofton Hall makes this blue cheese using unpasteurized milk from a single herd of Shorthorn cows. *Penicillium roqueforti* is added to the milk to create the veining, and the moulded curd is unpressed and pierced to encourage the mould to grow. The cheese is matured for five weeks and best eaten at six weeks. The texture is firm but buttery, and it has a nutty savouriness with a sharp after-tang.

SIZE	
D. 14cm (5½in)	
H. 7cm (2¾in)	
WEIGHT	
1kg (2¼lb)	
SHAPE Flat truckle	
MILK Unpasteurized cow's	
RENNET Vegetarian	
TYPE Modern	

BRENDON BLUE SOMERSET

This blue goat's cheese is made by the Exmoor Blue Cheese Company at Willett Farm, Lydeard St Lawrence, using goat's milk from local herds. *Penicillium roqueforti* is added to the milk to create the blue veining. Matured for four to six weeks, Brendon Blue has a natural rind over a white paste with a dryish, crumbly texture. The flavour combines a goaty freshness with a noticeable tang from the blue.

SIZE	
D. 11cm (4½in)	
H. 11cm (4½in)	
WEIGHT	
1kg (2¼lb)	
SHAPE Cylinder	
MILK Unpasteurized goat's	
RENNET Vegetarian	
TYPE Modern	

BUFFALO BLUE YORKSHIRE

One of a handful of British blue buffalo's milk cheeses, this is made by Shepherds Purse Cheeses, which sources its milk from a local farmer. Matured for 10 weeks, the cheese develops a brown rind, while the ivory paste is scattered with green-blue veining. The texture is soft and creamy, and the flavour of the paste is mild with a salty-nuttiness coming from the veining.

SIZE	
D. 20cm (8in)	
H. 20cm (8in)	
WEIGHT	
3kg (6½lb)	
SHAPE	Round
MILK	Pasteurized buffalo's
RENNET	Vegetarian
TYPE	Modern

CASHEL BLUE CO TIPPERARY

Named after the Rock of Cashel, this cheese was Ireland's first farmhouse blue cheese, created by the Grubbs in 1984. Today, the cheese is still made at their farm near Cashel using milk from their own cows as well as locally sourced milk. After maturing, the firm, moist cream-coloured paste is mottled with blue veining. Eaten at around three months, it has a melting, creamy texture and a mellow flavour.

SIZE	
D. 13cm (5in)	
H. 9cm (3½in)	
WEIGHT	
1.5kg (3lb 3oz)	
SHAPE	Round
MILK	Pasteurized cow's
RENNET	Vegetarian
TYPE	Modern

CORNISH BLUE CORNWALL

The Cornish Cheese Company makes this West Country cheese at its farm near Liskeard. *Penicillium roqueforti* is added at the start of the process, and the moulded, unpressed cheese is pierced to create the veining. Depending on the size of the cheese, it is matured for between 6–12 weeks. The resulting cheese has a creamy-textured pale yellow paste, blotched with blue veining, and a mild, sweet flavour.

SIZE
D. 10–28cm (4–11in)
H. 10–18cm (4–7in)
WEIGHT
500g–5kg (1lb 2oz–11lb)
SHAPE Round
MILK Pasteurized cow's
RENNET Vegetarian
TYPE Modern

CROZIER BLUE CO TIPPERARY

Available only seasonally, this cheese has been commercially produced since 1999 by the Grubb family at Beechmount near Fethard using locally sourced sheep's milk. A slow-maturing cheese, it has an ivory-coloured paste, crumbly when young, which becomes creamier as the cheese ages. The nutty sweetness of the sheep's milk contrasts with the spicy tang of the blue veining.

SIZE
D. 13cm (5in)
H. 9cm (3½in)
WEIGHT
1.5kg (3lb 3oz)
SHAPE Round
MILK Pasteurized sheep's
RENNET Vegetarian
TYPE Modern

DEVON BLUE DEVON

The Ticklemore Cheese Company makes a trio of blue cheeses using milk from different dairy animals, with this one made from locally sourced cow's milk. An unpressed cheese, it is matured until four months old. The resulting cheese has a crumbly, moist pale yellow paste, mottled with blue veining created by the addition of *Penicillium roqueforti*. The flavour is creamy with a rich savouriness.

SIZE	
D. 20cm (8in)	
H. 10–13cm (4–5in)	
WEIGHT	
3–3½kg (6½–7½lb)	
SHAPE Round	
MILK Pasteurized cow's	
RENNET Vegetarian	
TYPE Modern	

DORSET BLUE VINNEY DORSET

Mike Davies of Woodbridge Farm revived the making of this regional cheese (originally made using skimmed milk) in 1984. Today, his family continues to make it using hand-skimmed unpasteurized milk from the farm's cows, with additional skimmed milk powder. Matured for three to five months, it has a crumbly pale yellow paste, splotched with blue-green veins, and a mild, long-lasting savouriness.

SIZE	
D. 25cm (10in)	
H. 30cm (12in)	
WEIGHT	
6kg (13lb)	
SHAPE Truckle	
MILK Unpasteurized cow's	
RENNET Vegetarian	
TYPE Traditional	

BACTERIA AND MOULD

Bacteria and mould are generally viewed as something to be eliminated, which is why some people may not be comfortable with the idea that cheesemakers actively encourage the growth of certain moulds. Cheese is a fermented food and, in this carefully managed process of decay, bacteria and moulds play a vital role in creating flavour and texture.

To make blue cheeses, *Penicillium roqueforti* is added to the milk and encouraged to grow. The bloomy white mould rind on some cheeses is created through adding *Penicillium candidum*. A more unusual mould is *Geotrichum candidum*, which affects the cheese's flavour and texture. When making washed-rind cheeses, a solution containing *Brevibacterium linens* creates the characteristic pungent odour.

VEINING
The veining in blue cheese differs, but is always striking.

DUNSYRE BLUE LANARKSHIRE

Humphrey Errington of Walston Braehead Farm makes this blue cheese using unpasteurized Ayshire milk to which *Penicillium roqueforti* is added. The curd is cut, drained of whey, packed into moulds, rubbed with salt, pierced to let the veining develop, and matured for six weeks. The matured cheese has a creamy-textured pale yellow paste, blotched with blue-green moulding, which adds a powerful spiciness.

SIZE	
D. 16cm (6½in)	
H. 12cm (4¾in)	
WEIGHT	
3kg (6½lb)	
SHAPE Wheel	
MILK Unpasteurized cow's	
RENNET Vegetarian	
TYPE Modern	

EXMOOR BLUE SOMERSET

Made by Exmoor Blue Cheese Company at Willett Farm, this cheese uses locally sourced unpasteurized milk from Jersey cows – a fact assured by its Protected Geographical Indication (PGI) status, which defines how the cheese is made. Matured for four to six weeks, it develops a natural rind over a soft, blue-veined primrose yellow, paste. The sharp, tangy veining contrasts with the buttery creaminess of the paste.

SIZE	
D. 12cm (4¾in) & 18cm (7in)	
H. 6cm (2½in)	
WEIGHT	
500g (1lb 2oz) & 1.25kg (2¾lb)	
SHAPE Round	
MILK Unpasteurized cow's	
RENNET Vegetarian	
TYPE Modern	

FOWLERS FOREST BLUE
DERBYSHIRE

This cheese is made by Fowlers of Earlswood from pasteurized cow's milk. Matured in a humid environment for five months, it has a very thin, brown natural rind over a firm pale yellow paste, which is only lightly marked with green veining. The paste has a mild, salty flavour with a mild tang from the veining.

SIZE	
D. 20cm (8in)	
H. 15cm (6in)	
WEIGHT	
5kg (11lb)	
SHAPE Round	
MILK Pasteurized cow's	
RENNET Vegetarian	
TYPE Modern	

HARBOURNE BLUE DEVON

Robin Congdon makes this cheese at Ticklemore Cheeses, near Sharpham Barton, one of a trio of blue cheeses made from different milks. The milk used for this cheese comes from a local herd of goats reared outside, which adds complexity and interest to the flavour of their milk and hence to the cheese. Matured for four months, the ivory paste is streaked with blue-green veining, and it has a fruity, spicy flavour.

SIZE	
D. 20cm (8in)	
H. 10–13cm (4–5in)	
WEIGHT	
3–3.5kg (6½–7½lb)	
SHAPE Round	
MILK Pasteurized goat's	
RENNET Vegetarian	
TYPE Modern	

ISLE OF WIGHT BLUE
ISLE OF WIGHT

This cheese is made by the Isle of Wight Cheese Company using unpasteurized Guernsey milk from the dairy herd at the farm at which it is based. It is sold at four weeks, by which time it has a brown natural rind, blotched with mould, and a smooth creamy-textured paste. It has a nutty flavour and gentle bite from the veining.

SIZE	
D. 9cm (3½in)	
H. 4.5cm (1¾in)	
WEIGHT	
225g (8oz)	
SHAPE Round	
MILK Unpasteurized cow's	
RENNET Vegetarian	
TYPE Modern	

LANARK BLUE LANARKSHIRE

Humphrey Errington makes this cheese at Braehead of Walston using unpasteurized milk from his own ewes. *Penicillium roqueforti* is added to the warm milk at the start of the process. The curd is cut, drained of whey, packed into moulds, brined, salt-rubbed, and pierced to encourage the veining, then matured for six weeks. The pale ivory-coloured paste is mottled with blue-green veining and has a full, savoury flavour.

SIZE	
D. 16cm (6½in)	
H. 12cm (4¾in)	
WEIGHT	
3kg (6½lb)	
SHAPE Wheel	
MILK Unpasteurized sheep's	
RENNET Vegetarian	
TYPE Modern	

MRS BELL'S BLUE YORKSHIRE

This blue sheep's cheese is made by Shepherds Purse Cheeses of Thirsk using locally sourced milk, and is named after Judy Bell, who founded the company in 1987 on the Bells' farm. During maturing, the cheese develops a natural rind over a white paste, streaked with emphatic green-blue veins. The texture is soft and creamy with a sweet flavour, and there is only a mild tang from the blueing.

SIZE	
D. 20cm (8in)	
H. 18–20cm (7–8in)	
WEIGHT	
3kg (6½lb)	
SHAPE Wheel	
MILK Pasteurized sheep's	
RENNET Vegetarian	
TYPE Modern	

NANNY BLOO DEVON

Norsworthy Dairy in Crediton makes this blue cheese using unpasteurized goat's milk from its own mixed herd of Saanen, Toggenburg, and British Alpines. *Penicillium roqueforti* is added to the milk, and the cheese is spiked at three weeks to create the veining. Ready to eat at one month, the cheese has an orange-gold rind and mottled blue-green veining. The paste is soft and moist with a tongue-tingling tangy flavour.

SIZE	
D. 6cm (2½in)	
H. 10cm (4in)	
WEIGHT	
1.6–1.8kg (3¼–4lb)	
SHAPE Cylinder	
MILK Unpasteurized goat's	
RENNET Vegetarian	
TYPE Modern	

NEW FOREST BLUE WILTSHIRE

This blue cheese is made by Loosehanger Farmhouse Cheeses at Home Farm, Salisbury using milk from a single herd of Ayrshires. To create the blue veining, *Penicillium roqueforti* is added to the milk at the start of the process. The cheese is matured for 6–12 weeks, during which time it develops dark blue veining in a moist cream-coloured paste, which gives it a pleasant sharpness.

SIZE	
D. 15–17cm (6–6¾in)	
H. 11cm (4½in)	
WEIGHT	
1.3–1.5kg (3lb–3lb 3oz)	
SHAPE Cylinder	
MILK Pasteurized cow's	
RENNET Vegetarian	
TYPE Modern	

OLD SARUM WILTSHIRE

Loosehanger Farmhouse Cheeses makes this blue cheese using pasteurized milk from a single herd of Ayrshires. Taking as its inspiration the sweeter blue cheeses, Loosehanger uses a French version of a Dolcelatte mould to create the blueing. Ready to eat at six weeks, the cheese has a grey-brown natural rind and a yellow paste with green veining. The flavour is sweet and creamy with a gentle blue note.

SIZE	
D. 15–17cm (6–6¾in)	
H. 11cm (4½in)	
WEIGHT	
1.3–1.5kg (3lb–3lb 3oz)	
SHAPE Cylinder	
MILK Pasteurized cow's	
RENNET Vegetarian	
TYPE Modern	

PARTRIDGE'S BLUE SOMERSET

The Exmoor Blue Cheese Company at Willett Farm makes this blue cheese using locally sourced milk from Jersey cows. *Penicillium roqueforti* is added to the milk to create the veining, and the cheese is matured for six to eight weeks. It develops a natural rind over a pale yellow paste, intricately veined with blue-green mould. The texture is soft and creamy, and the flavour mellow with a savoury salty-sweetness.

SIZE	
D. 11cm (4½in)	
H. 10cm (4in)	
WEIGHT	
1.1kg (2½lb)	
SHAPE Drum	
MILK Unpasteurized cow's	
RENNET Vegetarian	
TYPE Modern	

PERL LAS DYFED

An organic blue cheese, this is made by Caws Cenarth at Glyneithinog Farm in Wales using cow's milk from Ffosyficer Organic farm. Matured for at least eight weeks, the cheese grows a pale gold natural rind, flecked with white, while the pale yellow paste is evenly veined with blue-green veining. When ripe, the paste becomes meltingly soft, while the flavour is salty and nutty with a mushroomy note from the veining.

SIZE	
D. 10cm (4in) & 20cm (8in)	
H. 8cm (3¼in) & 10cm (4in)	
WEIGHT	
450g (1lb) & 2.5kg (5½lb)	
SHAPE Round	
MILK Pasteurized organic cow's	
RENNET Vegetarian	
TYPE Modern	

PONT GAR BLUE CARMARTHENSHIRE

This small cheese is made in Wales by the Carmarthenshire Cheese Company based at Boksberg Hall, Llanllwch. It is a white mould-ripened cheese, and when matured the cheese's golden rind is coated with a bloomy white mould layer, caused by the *Penicillium candidum* added to the cheese. Inside, the glossy ivory-coloured paste is marked with a sprinkling of blue veining, adding a tang to the mild-flavoured cheese.

SIZE	
D. 10cm (4in)	
H. 3cm (1¼in)	
WEIGHT	
250g (9oz)	
SHAPE Round	
MILK Pasteurized cow's	
RENNET Vegetarian	
TYPE Modern	

QUANTOCK BLUE SOMERSET

The Exmoor Blue Cheese Company at Willett Farm, Lydeard St Lawrence, makes this blue cheese using locally sourced sheep's milk, to which *Penicillium candidum* is added. Matured for four to six weeks, the cheese has a natural rind over an ivory-coloured paste, splotched with green-blue mould. The cheese's texture is crumbly, while the flavour combines the sweet nuttiness of sheep's milk with a blue tang.

SIZE	
D. 11cm (4½in)	
H. 10cm (4in)	
WEIGHT	
1kg (2¼lb)	
SHAPE Drum	
MILK Unpasteurized sheep's	
RENNET Vegetarian	
TYPE Modern	

SHROPSHIRE BLUE
LEICESTERSHIRE

This cheese is not historically linked with Shropshire; it is, in fact, made by a number of the Stilton dairies. Colston Bassett makes the one shown, maturing it for six to eight weeks. Annatto is added to create the orange colour, while the veins are produced by adding *Penicillium roqueforti*. It has a firm but moist paste and a subtle, savoury flavour.

SIZE	
D. 20cm (8in)	
H. 25cm (10in)	
WEIGHT	
8kg (17½lb)	
SHAPE Cylinder	
MILK Pasteurized cow's	
RENNET Vegetarian	
TYPE Modern	

SOMERSET BLUE SOMERSET

This cheese is made by the Exmoor Blue Cheese Company at Willett Farm, Lydeard St Lawrence, using Jersey cow's milk sourced locally. The blue veining is created by the addition of *Penicillium candidum*. It is matured for five to six weeks, developing a tracing of blue-green veining through the creamy yellow paste. The texture is yielding while the spicy blueing contrasts with the butteriness of the rich Jersey milk.

SIZE	
D. 15cm (6in)	
H. 10cm (4in)	
WEIGHT	
2kg (4½lb)	
SHAPE Round	
MILK Unpasteurized cow's	
RENNET Vegetarian	
TYPE Modern	

STICHELTON NOTTINGHAMSHIRE

Randolph Hodgson of Neal's Yard Dairy and cheesemaker Joe Schneider have teamed up to create this blue cheese, made at the Stichelton Dairy, Collingthwaite Farm. Named after the original name of Stilton village, it is made using unpasteurized cow's milk from the farm, and traditional animal rennet. Matured for 12–14 weeks, it has a natural rind, a blue-veined yellow paste, and a savoury, lingering flavour.

SIZE	
D. 20cm (8in)	
H. 22cm (8½in)	
WEIGHT	
7kg (15½lb)	
SHAPE Cylinder	
MILK Unpasteurized cow's	
RENNET Traditional animal	
TYPE Modern	

STILTON LEICS, NOTTS, & DERBYS

Stilton, Britain's most famous blue cheese, has a venerable history. It was named after the town of Stilton, where at a busy stagecoach station on the Great North Road the enterprising landlord of the Bell Inn sold the cheese to appreciative travellers.

In the early 1720s the author Daniel Defoe wrote of passing through Stilton, which was, he noted, a town "famous for cheese". He went on to describe the cheese as follows: "It is called our English Parmesan, and is brought to table with the mites or maggots round it so thick that they bring a spoon with them for you to eat the mites with, as you do the cheese."

The fame of Stilton cheese during this period is attributed in part to Mrs Frances Pawlett of Wymondham in Leicestershire, a skilled cheesemaker, credited with doing much to rationalize the shape, size, and quality of the blue cheese made locally. This blue cheese was then supplied to Cooper Thornhill at the Bell Inn in Stilton, who became noted as the seller of the best blue cheese in the town.

A POPULAR CHEESE

Although the coming of the railways in the 1840s saw the collapse of the stage-coach business, the fame of Stilton cheese had spread, and it went on to attract an appreciative audience in London. It became particularly popular with members of the aristocracy, who visited nearby Melton Mowbray in Leicestershire to hunt. Its status as a staple of English food continues today, as Stilton remains a much-loved cheese across Britain, with national sales peaking at Christmas time.

made using animal or vegetable rennet

balance of flavours between blue veining and curd

COLSTON BASSETT STILTON

SIZE	
D. 20cm (8in)	
H. 19.5cm (7½in)	
WEIGHT	
7.8–8kg (17–17½ lb)	
SHAPE	Cylinder
MILK	Pasteurized cow's
RENNET	Traditional animal or vegetarian
TYPE	Traditional

creamy texture

COLSTON BASSETT STILTON
Among the smallest Stilton dairies, Colston Bassett near Nottingham has sourced its milk from the same farms since 1913. Great care is taken hand-ladling the curd into moulds. Matured for at least eight weeks, this Stilton has a mellow flavour and a hallmark creaminess.

A PROTECTED CHEESE

Unusually in the history of British cheeses, Stilton cheese was defined and protected early in the 20th century. In 1910 a group of Stilton cheesemakers set out a definitive process for making the cheese, and in 1969, when the cheesemakers sought legal protection for this method, a High Court judgment ruled as follows: "Stilton is a blue or white cheese made from full cream milk, with no applied pressure, forming its own crust or coat, and made in cylindrical form, the milk coming from English dairy herds in the district of Melton Mowbray and the surrounding areas of Leicestershire, Derbyshire, and Nottinghamshire."

Today, Stilton has the distinction of being one of the few British cheeses to be granted a Protected Designation Origin (PDO) status by the European Union. It must be made by only a licensed dairy in the counties of Derbyshire, Leicestershire, or Nottinghamshire from local pasteurized milk in a traditional cylindrical shape. It must be made to a traditional recipe, never pressed, and allowed to form its own crust. There are only seven UK dairies producing Stilton: Colston Bassett, Cropwell Bishop, Dairy Crest, Long Clawson, Quenby Hall, Tuxford & Tebbutt, and Websters. Together they produce more than a million Stilton cheeses each year.

THE PRODUCTION PROCESS

It takes 78 litres (137 pints) of milk to make one 8kg (17½lb) Stilton cheese. At the start of the process, the milk is mixed with a starter culture, a milk-clotting agent, and blue-mould spores (*Penicillium roqueforti*). The resulting curd is drained, cut, milled, and salted, and for each cheese around 11kg (24lb) of salted curd is placed in a cylindrical mould. This is drained naturally for five or six days, and turned daily to spread the moisture evenly. Crucially, Stilton is never pressed during the making process, allowing the cheese to develop the flaky, open texture essential for the blueing stage.

The drained cheeses are then sealed and ripened for a number of weeks, again being turned regularly; during this period they begin to form the classic Stilton crust. At about six weeks, the cheeses are pierced with long needles, allowing air to enter and the *Penicillum roqueforti* mould to grow, creating the characteristic blue-green veining. The Stilton cheeses leave the dairy at nine weeks, by which time their weight has reduced to around 8kg (17½lb) a cheese. The resulting Stilton has a blotched crust, a blue-veined paste, and a crumbly texture with a lasting, savoury taste. Longer maturing, for a further five to six weeks, results in a creamier texture and a mellower, fuller flavour. Although all seven Stilton dairies use the same overall techniques, the resulting cheeses vary noticeably in flavour and texture from dairy to dairy.

CROPWELL BISHOP STILTON
NOTTINGHAMSHIRE

Named after the village in which it is based, Cropwell Bishop Creamery sources the milk for its cheese from 10 core farms, with *Penicillium roqueforti* added to create the blueing. At its peak at 11 weeks, it has a distinctive pattern of blue-green veining with a rich but not overly assertive spicy flavour. Cropwell Bishop also produces an organic Stilton.

SIZE	
D. 20cm (8in)	
H. 25cm (10in)	
WEIGHT	
8kg (17½lb)	
SHAPE Cylinder	
MILK Pasteurized cow's	
RENNET Vegetarian	
TYPE Traditional	

QUENBY HALL STILTON
LEICESTERSHIRE

During the 18th century, the owner of Quenby Hall made a blue cheese, which was sold in Stilton. The current owner, Freddie de Lisle, has revived the tradition. Matured for up to 12 weeks, it has a textured natural rind and a firm yellow paste, mottled with blue-green veining. The texture is creamy and the flavour mild with a nutty tang.

SIZE	
D. 21cm (8¼in)	
H. 25 cm (10in)	
WEIGHT	
8–9kg (17½–20lb)	
SHAPE Cylinder	
MILK Pasteurized cow's	
RENNET Vegetarian	
TYPE Traditional	

STRATHDON BLUE ROSS-SHIRE

This blue cheese is made by Highland Fine Cheeses at Tain in Scotland. In order to retain the moisture in the curd, it is not scalded at all. The moulded cheese is matured for three months, developing a mould rind from the yeast still in the air from the dairy building's past as a brewery. It is a mild blue with a pale, moist veined paste, developing a long, peppery finish when older.

SIZE	
D. 30cm (12in)	
H. 10cm (4in)	
WEIGHT	
2.8kg (6¼lb)	
SHAPE Round	
MILK Pasteurized cow's	
RENNET Traditional animal & vegetarian	
TYPE Modern	

SUFFOLK BLUE SUFFOLK

The Suffolk Cheese Company makes this cheese using pasteurized milk from its herd of Guernsey cows and adding *Penicillium roqueforti* at the start of the making process. The unpressed, moulded curd is horizontally pierced and allowed to mature until it is four to five weeks old. The rich yellow of the Guernsey milk is reflected in the colour of the moist paste, while the flavour is creamy with a mellow blue note.

SIZE	
D. 10cm (4in)	
H. 7.5cm (3in)	
WEIGHT	
675g (1½lb)	
SHAPE Round	
MILK Pasteurized cow's	
RENNET Vegetarian	
TYPE Modern	

YORKSHIRE BLUE YORKSHIRE

Shepherds Purse Cheeses in Thirsk makes this blue cheese using locally sourced cow's milk. *Penicillium roqueforti* is added to the milk at the start of the cheese-making process to create the veining. Matured for 10 weeks, the Yorkshire Blue develops a natural rind over a pale yellow paste with blue-green veining. The texture is soft and creamy, and the cheese has a mellow flavour with a salty-nutty finish.

SIZE	
D. 20cm (8in)	
H. 20cm (8in)	
WEIGHT	
3kg (6½lb)	
SHAPE Round	
MILK Pasteurized cow's	
RENNET Vegetarian	
TYPE Modern	

ORGANIC CHEESES

The rise of interest in and demand for organic foods has led to an increasing number of organically certified cheeses being made in the United Kingdom. Whereas in 1994 only four organic cheeses were entered for the British Cheese Awards (see page 185), by 2007 there were 113 entries. For a cheese to be organic, it is not enough for it simply to be made from organic milk. The word "organic" is protected by EU law and covers both the raw materials and the processing, so the word is applied to how the cheese is made as well as what it is made from.

The Soil Association promotes sustainable organic farming and is the UK's largest organic certification body. Organic products must include no genetically modified (GM) organisms or their derivatives. Rennet produced from GM bacteria or fungi, therefore, is not permitted by the Soil Association, which stipulates that organic cheeses must use animal rennet or naturally occurring vegetarian rennet. It is possible to make organic cheeses using traditional calf rennet from non-organic calves.

GLOSSARY

Affinage: the process of ripening or maturing a cheese.

Annatto: a food colouring from the seeds of the annatto tree (*Bixa orellana*), traditionally used to add an orange colour to cheeses such as Red Leicester or Cheshire.

Biodynamic: a form of organic farming based on a holistic and spiritual understanding of nature.

Brevibacterium linens: an important surface-ripening bacteria used in cheesemaking.

Brining: soaking the cheese in a brine solution.

Curd: the solids created when the milk has been curdled.

Direct vat inoculation: freeze-dried starter cultures used to trigger the cheese-making process, which are added directly to the vat.

Geotrichum candidum: one of the moulds used to develop flavour and texture in cheese.

Lactic acid: the weak acid formed by the action of bacteria on lactose.

Lactose: sugar found naturally in milk.

Milling: the process of breaking the curd into small pieces.

Mould-ripened: a cheese into which moulds are introduced, to develop flavour and texture during ripening.

Protected Designation of Origin (PDO): a European Union system to protect a regional food produced in a given geographical area.

Protected Geographical Indication (PGI): a European Union system to protect a regional food with a link to a given geographical area.

Organic: a food sold as "organic" must be produced according to European laws on organic production, with growers, processors, and importers registered and approved by organic certification bodies.

Paste: the term used to describe the inside of a cheese.

Pasteurized: a term for milk that has been heat-treated, usually by heating it to 71.7°C (161°F) for 15 seconds, to kill naturally occurring micro-organisms that may cause disease.

Penicillium candidum: a mould used to create a bloomy white coating on cheese rinds. Also known as *Penicillium camemberti*.

Penicillium glaucum: a mould that is added to blue cheeses to create the blue-green veins.

Penicillium roqueforti: a mould added to create the blue-green veins in blue cheeses.

Pressing: a process during cheese-making when weight is applied to a moulded cheese to extract moisture and create texture.

Raw: describes milk that has not been heat-treated in any way.

Rennet: a substance used to curdle milk, made from animal, vegetarian, or genetically modified sources.

Scalding: heating the curd during cheese-making.

Starter: a mixture of bacteria used to raise the acid levels in milk.

Thermized: a method of heat-treating milk to kill any pathogens in it, using temperatures lower than pasteurization. The term applies to raw milk which has been heated for at least 15 seconds at a temperature between 57°C (135°F) and 68°C (154°F).

Thermophilic: literally "heat-loving", the term is used to describe both a heat-tolerant bacterial starter used in cheeses with a high cooking temperature, and a Swiss-style type of cheese made using such starters.

Traditional pint starter: a frozen bacterial culture, which must be diluted and incubated before use. It added to milk to trigger the first stages of the cheese-making process.

Triple-cream: describes soft cheeses made from milk with extra cream added.

Unpasteurized: a term to describe milk that has not been heat-treated in any way.

Washed-curd: describes a type of cheese made by washing the curd during the making process.

Washed-rind: a type of cheese made by washing the rind during maturing.

Whey: the watery element that remains liquid after milk has been curdled.

DIRECTORY OF RESOURCES

SPECIALIST CHEESE RETAILERS

ENGLAND
Ansteys
www.ansteys.com
St Peters Garden Centre
Norton
Worcestershire WR5 2NY
01905 353128

Arch House Deli
Arch House
Boyces Avenue
Bristol BS8 4AA
0117 974 1166

The Cheese Shop
116 Northgate Street
Chester
Cheshire CH1 2HT
01244 346240

The Cheeseboard
www.thecheeseboard.net
1 Commercial Street
Harrogate HG1 1 UB
01423 508 837

Cheeses
13 Fortis Green Road
Muswell Hill
London N10 3HP
020 8444 9141

Country Cheeses
www.countrycheeses.co.uk

Market Road
Tavistock
Devon PL19 0BW
01822 615035

26 Fore Street
Topsham
Devon EX3 9HD
01392 877746

1 Ticklemore Street
Totnes
Devon TQ9 5EJ
01803 865926

The Fine Cheese Company
www.finecheese.co.uk
29 & 31 Walcot Street
Bath
Somerset BA1 5BN
01225 483 407

La Fromagerie
www.lafromagerie.co.uk

2–6 Moxon Street
Westminster
London W1U 4EW
020 7935 0341

30 Highbury Park
Islington
London N5 2AA
020 7359 7440

Gog Magog Hills Farm Shop
www.gogmagoghills.com
Heath Farm
Shelford Bottom
Cambridge CB2 4AD
01223 248352

Hamish Johnston
www.hamishjohnston.com
63 Northcote Road,
London SW11 1PA
020 7738 0741

House of Cheese
www.houseofcheese.co.uk
13 Church Street
Tetbury GL8 8JG
01666 502865

Neal's Yard Dairy
www.nealsyarddairy.co.uk

17 Shorts Gardens
London WC2 9UP
020 7240 5700

6 Park Street
London SE1 9AB
020 7367 0799

Paxton & Whitfield
www.paxtonandwhitfield.co.uk

93 Jermyn Street
London SW1Y 6JE
020 7930 0259

1 John Street
Bath BA1 2JL
01225 466403

13 Wood Street
Stratford-upon-Avon
Warwickshire CV37 6JF
01789 415544

Rippon Cheese Stores
www.ripponcheese.com
26 Upper Tachbrook Street
London SW1V 1SW
020 7931 0628

Teddington Cheese
www.teddingtoncheese.co.uk

42 Station Road
Teddington
Middlesex TW11 9AA
020 8977 6868

74 Hill Rise
Richmond
Middlesex TW10 6UB
020 8948 5794

DIRECTORY OF RESOURCES

IRELAND
Sheridans Cheesemongers
www.sheridanscheesemongers.com

11 South Anne Street
Dublin
Republic of Ireland
+353 (0)1 679 3143

Pembroke Lane
Ballsbridge
Dublin
Republic of Ireland
+353 (0)1 660 8231

14–16 Churchyard Street
Galway
Republic of Ireland
+353 (0)91 564 829

Ardkeen Quality Food Store
Dunmore Road
Waterford
Republic of Ireland
+353 (0)51 874 620

SCOTLAND
Ian Mellis
www.ijmellischeesemonger.com

30a Victoria Street
Edinburgh EN1 2JW
0131 226 6215

205 Bruntsfield Place
Edinburgh EH10 4DH
0131 447 8889

6 Bakers Place
Stockbridge
Edinburgh EH3 6SY
0131 225 6566

Old Town Coffee Roasters
32 Victoria Street
Edinburgh EH1 2JH
0131 225 7497

492 Great Western Road
Glasgow G12 8EW
0141 339 8998

WALES
Blas ar Fwyd
www.blasarfwyd.com
Heol yr Orsaf
Llanrwst
Cymru LL26 0BT
01492 640215

Le Gallois Deli
231 Cathedral Road
Cardiff CF11 9PP
029 2023 5483

ON-LINE MAIL-ORDER RETAILERS

www.thecheesegig.com
Specialists in West Country cheeses, delivering to United Kingdom only.

www.thecheeseshed.com
Specialists in West Country cheeses, delivering to both the United Kingdom and Ireland.

www.countrycheeses.co.uk
Offer a wide selection, including cheese wedding "cakes", but deliver to the United Kingdom only.

www.elegusto.co.uk
A good selection of British and Continental wines and cheeses, delivered to United Kingdom only.

www.finecheese.co.uk
Offer cheeses, and accompaniments such as crackers, pickles, and fruit, delivering to the UK mainland only.

www.houseofcheese.co.uk
Deliver cheese and other fine foods to United Kingdom only.

www.teddingtoncheese.co.uk
Deliver a broad selection of cheeses to addresses worldwide.

OTHER SOURCES OF INFORMATION

The Cheese Web
Eclectic Events Ltd
Old Woolman's House
Hastings Hill, Churchill
Oxfordshire OX7 6NA
01608 659 325
www.thecheeseweb.com
(For details of the British Cheese Awards)

The Irish Farmhouse Cheesemakers Association
www.irishcheese.ie

Slow Food UK
Unit 3, Alliance Court
Eco Park Road
Ludlow
Shropshire SY8 1FB
01584 879559
www.slowfood.org.uk

Specialist Cheesemakers Association
17 Clerkenwell Green
London EC1R 0DP
020 7253 2114
www.specialistcheesemakers.co.uk

INDEX

INDEX

BIBLIOGRAPHY

Clifford, Sue & King, Angela, *England in Particular*, Hodder & Stoughton, London 2006

Davidson, Alan, *The Oxford Companion to Food*, Oxford University Press, Oxford, 1999

Freeman, Sarah, *The Real Cheese Companion*, Little, Brown & Company, London, 1998

Harbutt, Juliet, *Cheese*, Mitchell Beazley, London, 1999

Harbutt, Juliet, *Cheeses of the World*, Hermes House, London, 1999

Hickman, Trevor, *The History of Stilton Cheese*, Sutton Publishing, Stroud, 2005

Mason, Laura with Brown, Catherine, *Traditional Foods of Britain*, Prospect Books, Totnes, 1999

Masui, Kazuko & Yamada, Tomoko, *French Cheeses*, Dorling Kindersley, London, 1996

Michelson, Patricia, *The Cheese Room*, Penguin, London, 2005

Rance, Patrick, *The Great British Cheese Book*, Papermac, London, 1985

ACKNOWLEDGEMENTS

My heartfelt thanks, first of all, to the cheesemakers themselves, for their time and trouble in assisting me with this book, and also to the many wonderful cheesemongers and delicatessens who were fantastically helpful: Ian of the Cheese Shed; Elise and Gary Jungheim of Country Cheeses; the Fine Cheese Company; Patricia Michelson and Sarah Bilney at La Fromagerie; Mark Newman and Will Johnston of Hamish Johnston; Marc Kennard of Kennards; Randolph Hodgson and his great team at Neals Yard Dairy, with special thanks to Chris George, Michael Jones, Bronwen Percival, Sarah Stewart, and Martin Tkalez; Paxton and Whitfield; Philip and Karen Rippon and Jeremy of Rippon Cheese Stores; and Kevin Sheridan of Sheridan's Cheesemongers in Ireland. Putting a book together involves a lot of work from several people. My thanks for all their help and support to: Dawn Bates, Emma Forge and Tom Forge, Adèle Hayward, Will Heap, Stephanie Jackson, Kat Mead, Daniel Mills, Samantha Richards, Sara Robin, Siobhan Vorney, and Jenny Woodcock.

DK would like to thank Will Heap and Siobhan Vorney for their work on photography, and Randolph Hodgson and his team for permission to photograph at Neal's Yard Dairy.

PICTURE CREDITS

The publisher would like to thank the following for permission to reproduce photographs:
(Key: a-above; b-below/bottom; c-centre; l-left; r-right; t-top)

11 Getty Images: Chris Close. **13 Getty Images:** Brooke / Topical Press Agency. **15 britainonview.com:** Paul Felix. **16 britainonview.com:** Paul Felix. **17 Stilton Cheese Makers' Association – www.stiltoncheese.com. 23 4Corners Images:** Colin Dutton. **25 DK Images:** Ian O'Leary. **37 FLPA:** Nigel Cattlin. **52 Alamy Images:** Trevor Pearson (b). **72 FLPA:** John Eveson (b). **79 Alamy Images:** John Robertson (b). **110 FLPA:** Sunset. **125 Victoria Rance:** (b). **171 Stilton Cheese Makers' Association – www.stiltoncheese. com:** (b). **199 Alamy Images:** Bon Appetit (t)

All other images © Dorling Kindersley
For further information see: www.dkimages.com